W9-CBU-209

# Dementia

## Titles in the Diseases and Disorders series include:

# Dementia

## Lizabeth Hardman

**LUCENT BOOKS**
*A part of Gale, Cengage Learning*

GALE
CENGAGE Learning™

Detroit • New York • San Francisco • New Haven, Conn • Waterville, Maine • London

## GALE
CENGAGE Learning™

LIBRARY OF CONGRESS CATALOGING-IN-PUBLICATION DATA

Hardman, Lizabeth.
  Dementia / by Lizabeth Hardman.
    p. cm. – (Diseases and disorders)
  Includes bibliographical references and index.
  ISBN 978-1-4205-0042-4 (hardcover)
  1. Dementia–Juvenile literature. I. Title.
  RC521.H367 2009
  616.8'3–dc22

                                                          2008033856


Lucent Books
27500 Drake Rd.
Farmington Hills, MI 48331


ISBN-13: 978-1-4205-0042-4
ISBN-10: 1-4205-0042-2

Printed in the United States of America
2 3 4 5 6 7 12 11 10 09

Printed by Bang Printing, Brainerd, MN, 2nd Ptg., 10/2009

# Table of Contents

# "The Most Difficult Puzzles Ever Devised"

**C**harles Best, one of the pioneers in the search for a cure for diabetes, once explained what intrigued him so about medical research: "It's not just the gratification of knowing one is helping people," he confided, "although that probably is a more heroic and selfless motivation. Those feelings may enter in, but truly, what I find best is the feeling of going toe to toe with nature, of trying to solve the most difficult puzzles ever devised. The answers are there somewhere, those keys that will solve the puzzle and make the patient well. But how will those keys be found?"

Since the dawn of civilization, nothing has so puzzled people—and often frightened them, as well—as the onset of illness in a body or mind that seemed healthy before. Being unable to reverse conditions such as a seizure, the inability of a heart to pump, or the sudden deterioration of muscle tone in a small child, or even to understand why they occur was unspeakably frustrating to healers. Even before there were names for such conditions, before they were understood at all, each was a reminder of how complex the human body was and how vulnerable.

While our grappling with understanding diseases has been frustrating at times, it has also provided some of humankind's most heroic accomplishments. Alexander Fleming's accidental discovery in 1928 of a mold that could be turned into penicillin has resulted in the saving of untold millions of lives. The isolation of the enzyme insulin has reversed what was once a death sentence for anyone with diabetes. There also have been great strides in combating conditions for which there is not yet a cure. Medicines can help AIDS patients live longer, diagnostic tools such as mammography and ultrasounds can help doctors find tumors while they are treatable, and laser surgery techniques have made the most intricate, minute operations routine.

This "toe-to-toe" competition with diseases and disorders is even more remarkable when viewed in a historical continuum. An astonishing amount of progress has been made in a very short time. Just two hundred years ago, the existence of germs as a cause of some diseases was unknown. In fact, less than 150 years ago a British surgeon named Joseph Lister had difficulty persuading his fellow doctors that washing their hands before delivering a baby might increase the chances of a healthy delivery (especially if they had just attended to a diseased patient)!

Each book in Lucent's Diseases and Disorders series explores a disease or disorder and the knowledge that has been accumulated (or discarded) by doctors through the years. Each book also examines the tools used for pinpointing a diagnosis, as well as the various means that are used to treat or cure a disease. Finally, new ideas are presented—techniques or medicines that may be on the horizon.

Frustration and disappointment are still part of medicine because not every disease or condition can be cured or prevented. But the limitations of knowledge are constantly being pushed outward; the "most difficult puzzles ever devised" are finding challengers every day.

# The Memory Thief

It was November 1901, and Karl Deter of Germany did not know what to do about his wife, Auguste. Over the previous several months, her behavior had changed drastically. Only fifty-one years old, Auguste had lost the ability to remember things from one minute to the next. She had lost the ability to express herself with words. She was often confused about what day it was, where she was, and even who she was. She had frequent outbursts of anger and paranoid thinking. She would hide things, thinking her family was trying to steal from her. She could no longer take care of herself and needed constant care from her family. This was all very distressing because Auguste had always been healthy, with no history of any psychological problems.

Finally, following the advice of their family doctor, Karl brought his wife to the Asylum for the Insane and Epileptic in Frankfurt, Germany. The doctor's note read, in part, "Auguste D. has been suffering for a long time from weakening of memory, persecution mania, sleeplessness, restlessness. She is unable to perform any physical or mental work. Her condition needs treatment from the local mental institution."[1]

At the hospital, Auguste was examined by a psychiatrist named Alois Alzheimer. He asked her some questions. "What is your name?" he asked. "Auguste," she replied. "Last name?" "Auguste," she answered again. "What is your husband's name?" asked Dr. Alzheimer. "Auguste, I think," she replied. "How long have you been here?" She thought for a few moments.

"Three weeks." It was her second day there. Later she told Dr. Alzheimer, "I have lost myself."[2]

Over the next four years, Auguste's condition continued to worsen. She would scream almost constantly. She became more confused and no one could understand anything she said. She could not control her bowels or bladder. Eventually, she became bedridden and immobile. Finally, in April 1906, she died. She was only fifty-five years old.

During Auguste's hospitalization, Dr. Alzheimer kept very detailed notes about her illness. After she died, he examined tissues from her brain under a microscope. He discovered that the cells were shrunken, and contained strange clumps of brownish material. The clumps were found inside and between the nerve cells, interfering with their ability to send messages to each other. Dr. Alzheimer also observed what he called "a tangled bundle of fibrils," strands of ropelike threads that grew inside the cells. He wrote a paper about his findings called "Regarding a Curious Disease of the Cortex," and shared his discovery with his colleagues. One of them called the illness "Alzheimer's disease," and the name stuck. Dr. Alzheimer could not know at the time that his discovery would one day become the most common form of a pattern of symptoms called "dementia."

## A Long History

Dementia has been known since ancient times. Medical texts from the Roman Empire mention dementia. The Roman philosopher and politician Cicero wrote about it in the second century B.C., referring to it as "senilis stultitia." Even then, there was disagreement about whether it was an illness or a normal part of growing old. The word *dementia*, which comes from the Latin for "without mind," came into common use in the 1700s, and is mentioned in the 1808 code of law written by Napoleon Bonaparte.

Today, dementia in its various forms is diagnosed in almost 370,000 people in the United States each year. While older people make up the majority of those affected, people of any age can have it in one form or another. According to the Alzheimer's

Association, about 5 million Americans suffer from Alzheimer's disease alone. It ranks seventh among the leading causes of death in the United States. Many more people are affected by non-Alzheimer's dementias such as vascular dementia, caused by changes in the brain's blood supply, and frontotemporal dementia, which affects only certain parts of the brain. Still others have dementia as a result of brain infections or injuries. The U.S. Congress Office of Technology Assessment estimates that as many as 6.8 million Americans are affected with some form of dementia, 1.8 million of them severely.

## A Major Challenge

Dementia is like a thief. It robs people of their memories, their personalities, and their ability to care for themselves. Most

A daughter feeds oatmeal to her elderly mother, one of 5 million Americans stricken with Alzheimer's disease, the most common form of dementia.

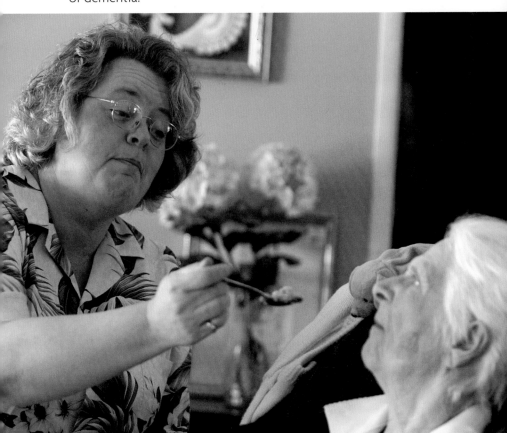

types of dementia are not curable or reversible. Many people with dementia eventually become completely dependent on others for their care, and it is the number-one reason for a person being placed in a nursing home or other institution. Dementia care can present significant emotional, physical, and financial challenges for families and all others who help care for them. It also places a huge financial strain on the health-care system. David Shenk, author of the book *The Forgetting: Alzheimer's, Portrait of an Epidemic*, writes in his article, "The Memory Hole,"

> The plodding progression of Alzheimer's devastates not only the patient but also a wide circle of family and friends forced to . . . participate in the long decline. The disease costs a fortune in medical and nursing fees and lost wages; a conservative estimate is that the current five million cases in the United States add up to more than $100 billion annually.[3]

Unlike other long-term illnesses, such as cancer and heart disease, which have been on the decline, dementias such as Alzheimer's disease are on the rise. Between 2000 and 2005, the incidence of Alzheimer's increased almost 50 percent. America's baby-boomer generation, those born between 1946 and 1964, are now entering the age at which people are at the highest risk of developing dementia—their late sixties and early seventies. As medical advances make it possible for people to live much longer into old age, the number of cases of dementia will continue to increase. "What we're faced with here is the boomer population coming of age," says Gary Small, director of the UCLA Center on Aging. "There are going to be a lot more people at risk."[4] A British study completed in early 2008 estimated that by the year 2040, there will be 81 million cases of dementia worldwide. Shenk paints an even grimmer picture. "By the middle of this century," he says, "15 million Americans could have Alzheimer's—about 100 million people worldwide—and national costs could reach $1 trillion."[5]

## Cause for Hope

The good news is that a great deal of research is being done in an effort to find better ways to prevent dementias, diagnose them earlier, and treat them more effectively. Scientists now understand dementia better than ever and, through educational efforts, are passing that understanding on to patients and those who care for them. Abundant sources of support and help exist for both patients and caregivers affected by dementia.

# CHAPTER ONE

# What Is Dementia?

**D**ementia is not so much a disease by itself but rather a set of symptoms that are caused by something going wrong in the brain. Many different cognitive functions, or mental abilities, can be affected by dementia. People with dementia may have trouble remembering things. They may not recognize people or places that they have known all their lives. They may wander away from home and have no idea how to get back. They may be unable to express or understand language. They may lose the ability to plan or organize things. Dementia can cause personality changes, turning a normally happy, peaceful person into an angry, hostile one, unable to control her emotions. People with dementia may eventually lose the ability to care for themselves, even to the point of having to be bathed, dressed, and fed by someone else.

Fifteen-year-old Laura describes what it was like when her grandmother developed Alzheimer's disease, the most common form of dementia:

> My mom first started to realize that something was different when she had to pick her up from the hospital after a fall that happened in her apartment. When she brought her home she found a whole bunch of boxes of junk. She also noticed that she wasn't paying her bills and was getting about a hundred magazine subscriptions that she wouldn't normally get. She was eating food that she didn't normally eat and her cupboards were filled with old, outdated food. Her apartment was not as clean as it

used to be, her driving was horrible, and she ran a stop sign and many other things that she wasn't supposed to do while driving. My mom took her to doctors to tell them what was happening and most said that it was normal forgetfulness.[6]

Dementia is most common in the elderly. For a long time it was called "senile dementia" or "organic brain syndrome," and was considered to be a normal part of aging. People with dementia were said to be senile, and very little was done to help the person or his family to cope with its effects. Now doctors and scientists understand that it is not at all a normal part of growing old, that it can occur in any age group, that it is caused by a number of medical conditions, and that there is much that can be done to help treat the symptoms and slow down their progression. What all types of dementias have in common is that they are all caused by problems in the brain.

## Dementia and the Brain

One expert, who writes about the brain, says,

> The healthy brain is very much alive. If you could see your brain, you would think that it looks quiet and more or less the same over large areas. But under the surface, your delicate brain is highly energetic. Electrical and chemical signals are traveling at unbelievable speeds among so many cells that your mind cannot begin to imagine what is going on inside your head. Inside your skull lies the most complex structure in the known universe.[7]

The brain is made up of over 100 billion nerve cells called neurons. It is like a master computer that runs every other part of the body and all its thousands of functions. Each body function is managed by a very specific part or parts of the brain, and damage to those parts will interfere with the particular functions that they manage. For example, damage to the back of the brain can cause vision problems. Speech is governed by one small area on the left side of the brain; understanding

# The Woman Who Could Not Forget

In 2000 a thirty-four-year-old woman now known only as "AJ" wrote to Dr. James McGaugh, one of the world's leading experts on memory, and told him about her uncanny ability to remember in extraordinary detail almost everything that has happened to her since the age of twelve. Given any date, she remembers what day of the week it was, what the weather was, what she did that day, and news events that happened on that day. AJ's memories come to her almost constantly and uncontrollably, like a movie of her whole life constantly playing in her head. At first, Dr. McGaugh was skeptical; many people had claimed to have extraordinary memories and later turned out to be fakes. But after meeting AJ and conducting careful examinations, he was convinced. He brought in two of his colleagues at the University of California, but after six years of interviews, brain scans, and tests, they were no closer to understanding how her memory could work the way it did. Her ability was so unique that they gave it a new name—hyperthymestic syndrome, from the Greek words *hyper* meaning "more than normal," and *thymesis* meaning "remembering."

In 2006 Brad Williams of Wisconsin read about AJ and realized that he had the same kind of ability. "I was sort of a human Google for my family," says Brad. "I've always been able to recall things." Says Brad's brother Eric, "All of us have the ability to store all this information and the difference with Brad is that he can retrieve it." Now Dr. McGaugh and his team are studying Brad, too. They hope that AJ and Brad will help them learn more about the way memory works, in order to help people who have problems with memory loss.

"Local Man Memory," WXOW News (LaCrosse, WI), January 19, 2008, http://www.wxow.com/Global/story.asp?s=8571632

speech is managed by another. Damage to either one of those areas affects ability to communicate with words. All forms of dementia result from the death of the brain's neurons or from interference with their ability to communicate with each other, and most are caused by damage in the part of the brain called the cerebral cortex.

## The Cerebral Cortex

The cerebral cortex is the largest part of the brain. It is the part most people visualize when they think of a brain. It lies just under the skull and covers most of the other deeper structures of the brain. The cortex plays a major role in important functions such as thinking, reasoning, attention, memory, speaking and understanding language, hearing, vision, taste, touch, smell, and consciousness.

A diagram of the human brain identifies the hippocampus, which is found on the inner side of the temporal lobes. Damage to the hippocampus results in memory loss, one of the most prominent symptoms of dementia.

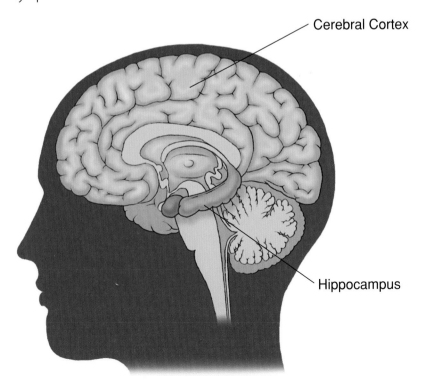

Cerebral Cortex

Hippocampus

The surface of the cortex is slightly grayish in color and is sometimes called "gray matter." The gray matter is made of millions of neurons. Neurons have long threadlike projections called axons that extend out from the main part of the neuron. Axons allow the neurons to connect with each other and communicate messages throughout the brain that tell the body what to do and how to do it. When a baby is born, not very many connections between neurons are made yet, but as a person learns new things by doing them over and over again—riding a bike, for example—more connections are made between the nerve cells. Soon, pathways are made that let the person do things and remember things without having to think about them very much. Each neuron can communicate with thousands or even tens of thousands of other neurons.

The cortex of the brain is divided into two halves, or hemispheres, the right and the left. The two hemispheres are connected to each other by a thick band of nerve fibers, called the corpus callosum, which allows the two hemispheres to send messages to each other. The right hemisphere controls the muscles on the left side of the body, and the left hemisphere controls the muscles on the right side. If a person sustains damage on one side of the brain, as in a stroke or head injury, movement on the opposite side is affected.

Most functions of the brain are carried out in both hemispheres, but some functions are managed mainly by one hemisphere or the other. For example, in most people, the ability to understand and express language is controlled by specific areas in the left hemisphere. The left hemisphere is also the center for precise skills such as math, logic, inventing, reasoning, and analyzing data to solve problems. The right side of the brain seems to be responsible for things such as recognizing faces, musical and artistic ability, and interpreting visual images.

The cerebral cortex is also divided into sections called lobes. There are four lobes in each hemisphere, each with its own special functions. The frontal lobes are located at the front of the brain, behind the forehead. They are responsible for individual personality, muscle movement, solving problems, making decisions and judgments, controlling behavior, emotions, and moods, and planning the future. The parietal lobes are located behind the frontal lobes at the top of the brain. They receive and process information sent to the brain by the senses, such as taste, vibrations, temperature, and pain. They also allow people to read, solve math problems, and have a sense of direction. The temporal lobes are on the sides of the brain behind the ears. They contain structures involved with emotions, hearing, language, and memory. The occipital lobe, located at the back of the head, is mainly the vision center.

## The Hippocampus

Besides the cerebral cortex, another part of the brain that is directly involved with dementia is the hippocampus. The hippocampus is located near the inner side of the temporal lobes. There is a hippocampus in each hemisphere. The hippocampus is necessary for forming new memories about events and facts. It also plays a part in holding on to the memories that are formed. Damage to the hippocampus makes it almost impossible for a person to form new memories. It also causes problems in recalling memories that were made before the damage occurred. In most people with dementia, the first and most noticeable sign is loss of memory.

## Dementia and Memory

Memory is a complex brain function that is controlled by several structures in the brain, along with the hippocampus. There are several different kinds of memory. In general terms, memories can be classified as either declarative or nondeclarative. Declarative memory, sometimes called episodic memory, involves remembering specific places and times, or episodes, in a person's life. The episodes may be recent, or they may have happened a long time ago. Examples of a declarative memory would be what a person did on his last vacation or who he had dinner with last Sunday. Declarative memories are formed in the hippocampus. In Alzheimer's disease, declarative memory is often severely

The human brain generates several different types of memory. Remote memory involves the ability to recall people and events from long ago, such as those that might be captured in an old photograph.

affected because of the damage the disease does to the hippocampus.

The other broad category of memory is nondeclarative memory, also called semantic memory. This type of memory is more subconscious than declarative memory. Rather than relating to specific events or people, it involves such things as knowing how to play a video game or ride a bike or recite a nursery rhyme, even if the person does not remember exactly how or when he learned those skills. It allows people to understand the meanings of things they have heard or seen before, such as what an ambulance siren means or what a fork is for.

Two other types of memory are remote memory and short-term memory. Remote memory is the memory of events that happened very long ago, such an elderly couple's memories of their wedding day fifty years ago. Short-term memory is memory of very recent things. A person with short-term memory loss may ask a question that he just asked a few minutes earlier, or he may forget why he came into a room, or what he had for lunch that afternoon. Short-term memory loss is an early symptom of dementia and is usually the first symptom noticed by the person with dementia or his family.

Another more specific type of memory is working memory. Working memory is a kind of very short-term memory used when a person must retain a small bit of information for a short time only until it is needed. An example is being told a phone number and remembering it only long enough to call the number. Working memory has a limited capacity, allowing only a few bits of information to be stored there at one time. Working memory is managed mainly by the frontal and parietal lobes.

## General Symptoms of Dementia

The cerebral cortex is involved with many different functions of the brain besides memory, all of which also have important roles in a person's ability to manage the activities of daily life. Because of this, damage to the cortex can cause lots of different kinds of symptoms. The particular symptoms that show vary from person to person depending on the cause of the dementia, what parts of the brain are affected, and on how far the dementia has progressed. A person may have many symptoms or just a few. Sometimes the symptoms are obvious. Other times, they are more subtle and may go unnoticed for years. As dementia progresses from early dementia through intermediate dementia to severe dementia, the symptoms become progressively worse and more difficult to manage.

## Early Dementia

The first sign of dementia is usually difficulty with short-term memory, but there are other signs that may become noticeable. The person may have increasing difficulty remembering words and might compensate for it by using a different word to say what he means. He may forget appointments or people's names. He may have problems with everyday tasks such as driving, managing his bank account, or preparing a meal. Gloria recalls the signs of early Alzheimer's disease in her husband: "The first time I really began to notice there was a problem

Frustration, confusion, and anger are common reactions of those in the early stages of dementia, as they find themselves increasingly forgetful or unable to manage everyday tasks.

was one day when he tried to install a screen in the door. He stood there with the screen in his hand, looking at the frame, and said to me, 'I can't figure out how to do this.' I recalled that months earlier, he had also said it was getting hard to balance the checkbook and had asked me to figure it out."[8]

The person in the early stages of dementia may become frustrated because of these problems and may show unusual anger or other changes in mood or personality. He may withdraw from others and become more isolated from friends and family. He may become paranoid, believing that loved ones are plotting things behind his back. Familiar surroundings may seem completely unfamiliar, and he may wander off and get lost, looking for something he can recognize.

## Intermediate Dementia

As the disease causing the dementia worsens, so do the symptoms. The person finds that he is no longer able to compensate for his memory problems. He may be unable to learn new things. He may lose his ability to feed, dress, or bathe himself. He may experience sleep disturbances, sleeping during the day and staying awake all night. His confusion and inability to recognize familiar surroundings and people gets worse. The person in intermediate dementia is at increased risk of falling because of confusion and problems with balance. Mood swings become more pronounced, with anxiety, depression, anger, and paranoia. He may also have hallucinations—believing that objects he sees are really something else. He may also have delusions—thinking things that cannot be true or believing that things have happened that never really happened.

## Severe Dementia

As the disease progresses from intermediate into severe dementia, these symptoms continue to worsen. The person may become completely dependent on others for all his care. He may be unable to walk or even get out of bed. He may lose the ability to control bowel or bladder function. He may have

A woman with severe dementia rocks in her chair at a nursing home. People in the advanced stages of dementia require intensive, constant care, as the disease that initially affected their mental functions ultimately impairs their ability to breathe, eat, and move.

trouble swallowing, and may choke on food and liquids. If the person gets food, liquids, or saliva in his lungs, he may develop pneumonia and have trouble breathing. He may become dehydrated or malnourished and require placement of a feeding tube into his stomach or small intestine. As a result of prolonged inability to move, the skin may break down and cause bedsores. In these last stages of dementia, death results, often from infections in the lungs or the blood.

## Risk Factors for Dementia

These symptoms of dementia are life changing for the patient and all those involved in his life. It is almost impossible to predict who will develop dementia and who will not, but there are risk factors that can make it more likely that a person will develop some form of dementia at some time during his life. Some of the risk factors can be modified, or changed, to reduce their risk; others cannot.

One of the most important and unchangeable risk factors for dementia is age. As a person gets older, changes in the brain occur that make it more likely that a person will develop at least some dementia symptoms. The risk of dementia due to Alzheimer's disease goes up rapidly as a person ages. After age sixty-five, the percentage of people with dementia doubles with every decade of life. Of the approximately 5.2 million Americans with Alzheimer's, about 5 million of them, or 96 percent, are over sixty-five, and in people over ninety, Alzheimer's accounts for 80 percent of all dementias.

## Dementia and Genetics

Another unchangeable risk factor for dementia is genetics. Scientists have identified several genes that seem to increase a person's chances of developing certain kinds of dementia. For example, Huntington's disease, which causes a severe dementia, is known to be caused by a defective gene located on chromosome 4. A genetic defect is also responsible for Niemann-Pick disease, which in its later stages can cause dementia in children.

Mutations, or changes, in three genes associated with Alzheimer's seem to cause the disease to start earlier than usual, before age sixty-five. Doctors refer to this as early onset

# Split-Brain Surgery

Split-brain surgery was originally done as a way to control severe epilepsy, a disease that causes seizures. In epilepsy, abnormal neurons in one hemisphere start firing messages to other neurons in an uncontrolled way, called a "storm," causing the body to have a seizure. In the worst kinds of epilepsy, the storm crosses to the other hemisphere, the entire brain becomes involved, and a grand mal seizure results. The person's body becomes stiff and shakes uncontrollably. The person may even stop breathing. If a seizure happens while a person is driving or doing other such activities, serious injuries can result.

Split-brain surgery involves cutting the corpus callosum, the part of the brain that connects the two hemispheres and allows them to send messages to each other. When the surgery is done, the two hemispheres cannot fully communicate with each other. This prevents the storm from crossing hemispheres and helps control the seizures.

People who have this surgery usually do not show any abnormal behavior afterward, but they do show signs that the hemispheres are not communicating. For example, if the person looks at a blank screen, and a picture of an object is very quickly flashed on the left side of the screen, that information is sent to the left hemisphere, and the person can name the object because the speech centers are located in the left hemisphere. But if the picture is flashed on the right side of the screen, the information stays in the right hemisphere. The person says they saw nothing, because the right hemisphere has no speech center and cannot "talk," and it can no longer send the information over to the left hemisphere.

Alzheimer's. These genes are called deterministic genes, meaning that inheriting even just one of the three genes from either parent is highly likely to cause early onset symptoms. James S. was an information technology director for a Fortune 500 company, only in his forties, when symptoms started to show. He says, "People would ask me, they would say, 'Well, why weren't you at the meeting?' And I said, 'Well, there was no meeting that I'm aware of.' And they said, 'Well, you called the meeting. You should be aware of it.'"[9]

Changes in another gene, called the apolipoprotein E (apoE) gene, can cause later-onset Alzheimer's. One version of the apoE gene, called apoE e4, especially affects men. In January 2007 researchers discovered another gene, called SORL1, which is also linked to later-onset Alzheimer's. These genes are called risk genes, meaning that inheriting them increases the risk, but does not guarantee it. In addition to the apoE and SORL1 genes, scientists believe there may be many more risk genes not yet discovered.

People with a parent or sibling with Alzheimer's are two to three times more likely to get it than those with no affected family members. A study published in 2008 found that children whose parents both had Alzheimer's disease were especially at risk. "There probably is an increased risk for Alzheimer's disease in the children of spouses that both have the disease," says Dr. Thomas D. Bird, the leader of the research team. Some people with a strong family history of dementia never develop it, however, and others with no family history at all may get it. "The exact magnitude of the risk, we don't know yet," says Dr. Bird. "There were ninety-eight children [in the study group] who had gotten to age seventy, and of that group, forty-one had developed Alzheimer's disease. That's about forty-two percent. We felt that's pretty important."[10]

## Controllable Risk Factors

One risk factor for dementia that people can control is the abuse of tobacco. Highly toxic chemicals in cigarette smoke can damage the small, very delicate blood vessels that carry

Excessive consumption of alcohol can permanently damage a person's brain cells, resulting in alcohol dementia. As with vascular dementia, which can occur among smokers, alcohol dementia is preventable.

oxygen-rich blood to the central parts of the brain. Lack of blood supply damages the brain cells, which leads to the second most-common type of dementia, called vascular dementia. This kind of dementia is also more common in people with diabetes, high blood pressure, high cholesterol, and obesity.

Researchers have found that the abuse of alcohol can also damage brain cells and can cause personality changes and problems with learning, judgment, decision making, and memory. Doctors call this type of dementia alcohol dementia. As with smoking, the dementia caused by alcohol abuse can be permanent. These controllable risk factors can be modified and their risk decreased by avoiding alcohol and tobacco abuse, by eating a healthy diet, and by getting regular exercise.

# CHAPTER TWO

# What Causes Dementia?

**D**ementia, because it is a group of symptoms rather than one disease, has many different causes. One way doctors classify dementias is by the location in the brain of the specific disease that is causing the dementia. If the disease is in the cerebral cortex, it is called cortical. If it is somewhere in the brain below the cortex, it is called subcortical. With treatment, some causes are reversible to some extent. Others are irreversible and progressive, meaning that the symptoms will get worse over time even with treatment. The most common form of dementia, Alzheimer's disease (AD), is responsible for about half of all cases of dementia. It is irreversible, progressive, and causes damage in both cortical and subcortical areas of the brain.

## Alzheimer's Disease

Kris was a forty-six-year-old mother and wife, healthy, active, and happy in her job, looking forward to her husband's retirement, when she began to notice some changes. She says,

> I started to become forgetful, which was not like me at all. I had an almost photographic memory and relied on that all my life. I had a very stressful job and worked long hours, so I blamed that for my forgetfulness. I couldn't remember things like my home phone number, my associates' names, or, on bad days, how to get home. I remember that many times I would

stop at a gas station, and after filling my tank, not knowing whether I was going to work or coming home from work. One day in December, my husband and I were out shopping, and he went to a different department in the store. The next thing I knew is that I couldn't remember where I was or how I had gotten there. It was time to fess up.[11]

Kris had tried to hide her symptoms, but it became too difficult. She finally sought medical attention, and after many tests, was diagnosed with early onset AD.

## The Progression of AD

Except for the young age at which they started, Kris's early symptoms were typical of AD. Like Kris, many people experiencing mild memory loss, especially for recent events or recently

For someone with Alzheimer's disease, what begins as occasional memory loss soon progresses into more serious cognitive difficulties and behavioral changes that can leave the person confused and unable to care for himself.

learned things, tend to dismiss it as just being stressed or "part of getting old." But, as in Kris's case, the signs get worse over time as other problems begin to emerge. Whole conversations may be entirely forgotten. Other cognitive skills then begin to weaken. For example, the person may become disoriented and not know what day it is, where he is, or how to get home, even if he already is home. There may be problems with language as the person struggles to find the words he wants to say.

Later, the person may not recognize familiar people, even his own children. Inability to plan or organize may mean that bills do not get paid and appointments get missed. He may believe others are stealing from him, or that family members have been replaced by strangers. He may become verbally or physically aggressive or believe that things that never happened actually did happen. He may stop taking care of himself, forgetting to bathe or eat. He may lose the ability to do basic everyday skills such as cooking, cleaning, or taking care of pets. Eventually, he is likely to need complete, round-the-clock care from others.

## Plaques and Tangles

These symptoms of AD are the result of significant changes in the brain. When Dr. Alois Alzheimer, for whom AD was named, first began to study the disease in the early 1900s, he learned a great deal about it from microscopic examinations of the brains of people who had died from early onset dementia. He noted dark "peculiar material"[12] both inside and around the neurons in the brain. Later researchers discovered that the dark material consisted of abnormal clumps, or aggregates, of proteins that are normally found in the brain. The protein aggregates were found to be toxic to nerve cells and caused them to malfunction and then to die. Other kinds of protein aggregates are known to cause other diseases besides AD, such as the muscle-wasting disease amyotrophic lateral sclerosis (ALS, also known as Lou Gehrig's disease) and the blood disorder sickle cell disease.

Two kinds of protein abnormalities in the brain are associated with AD. The first is called beta amyloid plaques. Beta amy-

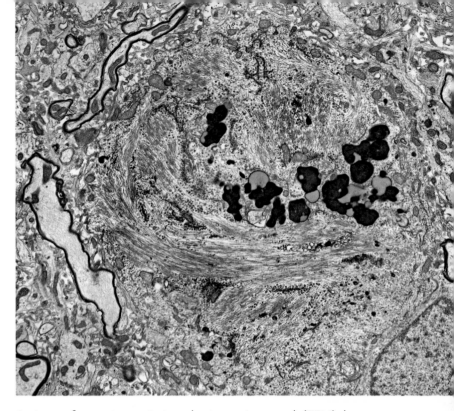

An image from a transmission electron micrograph (TEM) shows a neurofibrillary tangle, colored green, in a nerve cell from a person with Alzheimer's disease. The tangle consists of abnormal aggregates of tau protein.

loid is a protein that is normally found in the body. It is formed when a much longer protein molecule called amyloid precursor protein (APP) is cut into pieces by an enzyme—a chemical that breaks down other chemicals. Normally, beta amyloid in the brain is flushed out of the neurons and removed from the brain. In Alzheimer's disease, however, fragments of beta amyloid stick to each other, which creates abnormal clumps, or plaques, that collect between the neurons. Beta amyloid plaques interfere with the ability of the neurons to communicate with each other and eventually destroy them.

The other protein abnormality is called neurofibrillary tangles. Tangles are made mostly of another protein called tau protein. In normal neurons, tau protein helps support the neuron's structure and helps deliver chemical substances throughout the neuron. In AD, however, the tau becomes twisted into threads

# Dr. Alois Alzheimer

Alois Alzheimer was born on June 14, 1864, in Bavaria, a region of southern Germany. In school he was very good at science and graduated with a medical degree in 1887. He went to work at the state asylum for the mentally ill in Frankfurt and became interested in studying the cerebral cortex of the brain. He also began studying psychiatry and brain disorders.

During the next several years, Alzheimer worked with neurologist Franz Nissl and wrote a six-volume work about disorders of the nervous system. In 1895 he became director of the asylum, but continued his work on psychiatric illnesses such as schizophrenia and manic depression. He wanted to spend more time in research and patient care, so in 1903 he took a position as a research assistant at the medical school in Munich. He published many research papers about diseases of the brain, and soon he became well known among others in his field. He also gave many talks, and in 1906 he gave a talk in which he described "an unusual disease of the cortex," the disease that his patient Auguste D. had, and which his colleague Emil Kraepelin named "Alzheimer's disease."

In 1912, Alzheimer was appointed professor of psychiatry at the University of Breslau. On the train to Breslau, he became ill with a serious respiratory illness which eventually damaged his heart. He died in 1915. He was only fifty-one years old.

Dr. Alois Alzheimer was a German psychiatrist in the late 1800s and early 1900s who studied various neurological disorders, ultimately identifying the physiological characteristics of the disease that now bears his name.

that bunch together into tangles. Tangles are found inside the cells, rather than between them. Like amyloid plaques, tangles damage the structure of the neurons and prevent them from transporting messages properly, and eventually they die.

Autopsies have shown that most people who live into old age develop some protein plaques and tangles, but the brains of Alzheimer's patients have many more than those who do not have AD. Researchers are not entirely sure if the plaques and tangles actually cause AD, or if AD causes the plaques and tangles which then damage the brain and cause the symptoms. They do know, however, that plaques and tangles increase in number throughout the brain as the disease progresses.

## Lewy Body Dementia

AD is the most common form of dementia, but it is by no means the only kind. After Alzheimer's disease, Lewy body dementia is the second most-common kind of dementia in elderly people. It is also one of the most frightening types of dementia and can be very difficult to deal with. Like AD, Lewy body dementia is also caused by abnormal deposits of protein in the nucleus of the neurons. These deposits are called Lewy bodies, after Dr. Friedrich Lewy, who first discovered them in 1912. Lewy bodies are smooth, round clumps of protein that appear mainly in the cerebral cortex but are also found in deeper parts of the affected brain. No one knows yet what causes the bodies to form in the brain, but, like other dementias, it is thought to be a genetic malfunction.

Lewy body dementia can occur by itself, or it can occur along with AD or another brain disease called Parkinson's disease. Lewy bodies have been found in the brains of people with these two diseases, and some of the symptoms of Lewy body dementia are very similar to their symptoms, such as the memory loss of AD or the muscle stiffness and shakiness of Parkinson's disease.

One of the common early signs of Lewy body dementia is detailed visual hallucinations. One woman whose mother has Lewy body dementia describes what this was like for her mother:

Her hallucinations have been getting worse and worse. She is extremely afraid of snakes and this spring started seeing them everywhere inside and outside of the house. Of course there are people in the trees, on the rooftops, horses and mules in the trees, etc. She has a little man with silver toes that sleeps on the end of her bed each night. At first she was afraid of him but I have convinced her that he is an angel there to protect her and so she seems better with that.[13]

Another person whose father had Lewy body dementia writes, "This past November 2006 . . . he said he was seeing bugs. They were very vivid to him—even sitting on furniture." After having anesthesia for surgery, it got worse. "He started to think someone was trying to steal his car. Silk flowers had faces. Kids were in the house. There were two of my brother, two of my mom, two of me, and two houses. Also, little robot things were in the house, people were in the trees and machines like go-carts were in neighbors' back yards."[14]

The person with this type of dementia may also have hallucinations involving other senses, such as hearing sounds or smelling odors that are not there. They may also have delusions—thinking things that cannot possibly be true. The symptoms of Lewy body dementia tend to come and go, and the person may have "good" days, when he appears normal, followed by "bad" days, when he is confused, disoriented, and having hallucinations or delusions. At this time, there is no cure for Lewy body dementia.

## Vascular Dementia

After AD, the second most-common form of dementia in people of all ages is vascular dementia (VaD). It accounts for about 20 to 40 percent of all dementias, and more than a million Americans have it. It is most common in people who also have high blood pressure, high cholesterol, heart disease, diabetes, and alcoholism, and in people who smoke. It is more common in men than in women.

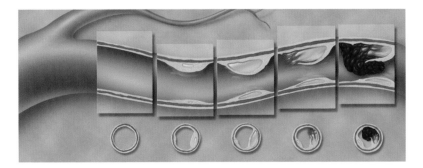

A five-part illustration shows the progression of atherosclerosis, which is caused when deposits of various substances build up within the artery over time, eventually causing a blockage that slows or prohibits the flow of blood.

Symptoms of vascular dementia can be very similar to AD, but the cause is very different. "Alzheimer's is more closely related to a build-up of plaques and tangles in the brain," says Dr. Murali Doraiswamy of Duke University Medical Center. "In vascular dementia it's more a blockage in the brain."[15] Vascular dementia results when the arteries that carry blood to the brain become blocked with deposits of a fatty substance called cholesterol, dead blood cells, and other substances, which interfere with the brain's blood supply. The deposits also cause the walls of the arteries to become thick and rigid, a condition called atherosclerosis, once called "hardening of the arteries." These changes can slow or even completely cut off blood flow to the part of the brain supplied by the clogged artery. Blockage of an artery is called an infarction, so VaD is also sometimes called multi-infarct dementia.

If an infarction happens suddenly in the brain, the person may have a stroke. A stroke happens when the supply of blood to a part of the brain is suddenly cut off. The person having a stroke may experience sudden weakness on one side of his body, slurred speech, visual disturbances, or other symptoms, depending on which part of the brain is affected by the stroke. Depending on how quickly the person gets medical attention and on how much of the brain is damaged by the stroke, the damage may be permanent, with signs of dementia.

# Prion Diseases

Prion diseases are a group of rare diseases that affect the nervous system in both humans and animals, mainly cows, sheep, and wild deer. The so-called mad cow disease is a prion disease of cattle. A common human form is Creutzfeldt-Jakob disease (CJD). Prion diseases impair brain function and, in people, cause dementia-like symptoms such as memory loss, changes in personality, and problems with learning and movement. The symptoms worsen over time, and they are usually fatal within weeks or months.

A prion is a very small piece of abnormal protein material that has become infectious, like a bacteria or a virus, and can cause illness. Prions are created when a mutation in a gene causes the formation of an abnormal protein called PrPsc. The abnormal PrPsc protein forms clumps that build up in the brain in a way similar to the protein plaques seen in Alzheimer's disease and other dementias. The clumps destroy nerve cells and form holes in the brain tissue. Prion diseases are interesting to scientists because the abnormal protein can actually behave like a germ, infecting normal protein and turning it into abnormal protein.

Because prion diseases are caused by a genetic mutation, they can be inherited from parents. Most cases are not inherited, however, but occur from exposure to outside sources of the abnormal protein. For example, people can get CJD from eating beef from cows that have mad cow disease. Prion diseases are also interesting to scientists because they are the only known diseases that are both hereditary and infectious at the same time.

If the changes in the blood vessels happen over a longer time, the person may have a series of very small strokes, or "silent" strokes, that he may not even notice, but they can damage the brain even before the person even shows any symptoms. Professor of psychology Shari Waldstein says, "People with stiffening of their arteries show a decline in memory and concentration as they grow older. Arterial stiffening negatively impacts cognitive performance before people have a stroke or develop dementia."[16] Eventually, as more and more small vessels get blocked, the damage to the brain gets worse, and he begins to have symptoms similar to Alzheimer's, with worsening memory and loss of cognitive functions.

It can be difficult to tell for certain whether a person has AD or vascular dementia because the symptoms are so similar. It is also possible for a person to have both diseases at once, which makes correct diagnosis even harder. Says Dr. Heidi Roth of the University of North Carolina at Chapel Hill, "One third of people with Alzheimer's disease may have a vascular component, and one third of people with vascular dementia may have Alzheimer's disease."[17] One difference between vascular dementia and AD is in how the disease first shows itself. Says Dr. Doraiswamy, "In Alzheimer's disease, typically you have memory loss as the initial presenting feature. That may be the case in vascular dementia, but it depends on where the stroke occurs; you might have a speech problem first."[18] People with vascular dementia often have problems with balance, movement, and shakiness earlier on in the disease process than those with AD. If they have personality changes, they tend to occur later in the disease than in AD. Another difference is that in vascular dementia, the symptoms may seem to worsen in a stepwise fashion, getting worse after each small stroke, rather than gradually as in AD. If the health issues that lead to atherosclerosis are treated early, the symptoms of vascular dementia can be slowed down, but once function is lost, it cannot be regained.

## Frontotemporal Dementia

Frontotemporal dementia (FTD) is the name given to a group of diseases that, like vascular dementia, may be mistaken for AD. Because of its early symptoms, FTD may also be misdiagnosed as a mental illness, such as depression, bipolar disorder, or schizophrenia. FTD can start anywhere from age thirty-five to about seventy-five. Both men and women are affected equally.

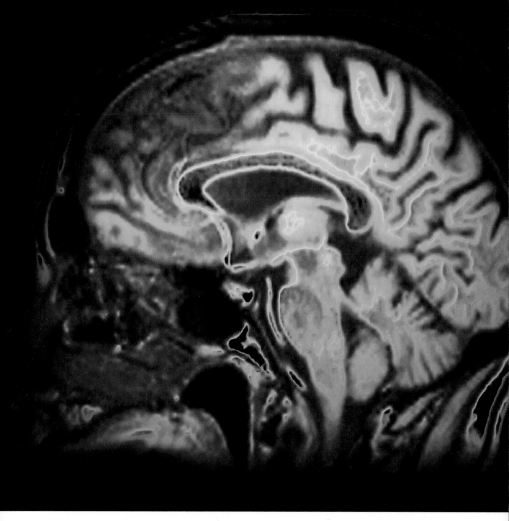

A magnetic resonance imaging (MRI) scan shows the brain of a fifty-year-old patient whose frontal and temporal lobes are shrunken, resulting in frontotemporal dementia.

Slightly less than half of FTD patients have it in their family, and some types of FTD, about 40 percent of cases, are caused by genetic abnormalities.

Doctors have learned much of what they know about FTD by examining the brain tissue of people who have died from FTD. In about 25 percent of cases, the nerve cells of the brain contain abnormal protein deposits inside them called Pick bodies. Others show signs of the same tangles of tau protein found in brains of AD patients. These disorders usually affect the frontal lobes and the front part of the temporal lobes of the brain, which begin to atrophy, or shrink in size, with loss of nerve cells in those lobes. These lobes are responsible for personality, behavior, and language, and damage to them shows in the symptoms.

Unlike AD, which typically starts with memory loss, FTD usually begins with noticeable changes in behavior, especially social behavior. People with FTD may use inappropriate language, have outbursts of anger and aggression, or be very rude. As the disease progresses, they may stop caring about their appearance or their hygiene, and stop bathing or brushing their teeth and hair. They may start to overeat to an extreme or develop obsessions with eating only certain foods. Another sign unique to FTD is repetitive behavior—doing certain things over and over again. The person with FTD usually seems to be aware that he is behaving strangely, but if someone points it out to him, he may not seem to care.

Another less common sign of some types of FTD is called progressive nonfluent aphasia, and has to do with language. The person may often use the wrong word to name an object, or may have difficulty expressing himself with words. As the disease worsens, the person uses less and less language, and may eventually stop speaking altogether. Other people with FTD have what is called semantic dementia, in which they may use correct words and grammar, but the things they say may have no meaning to them, or have nothing to do with the conversation at the time. Later on, they may have difficulty with reading and writing or may not remember what an object is used for.

## Dementias in Children

All these forms of dementia are found mostly in adults, but certain kinds of dementia are unique to children. When Jessica L. was just two months old, she was found to have a slightly enlarged liver. After more tests were done, including genetic tests, Jessica was diagnosed with a hereditary disease called Niemann-Pick disease (NP). There are four kinds of Niemann-Pick disease, type A, B, C, and D. Jessica's was type C. As she grew, she looked normal, but developed slowly. She began to have trouble with schoolwork and struggled in her ballet class. "Her last recital I could tell the difference," says her mother Lisa. "She knew every step, but her timing was off." Then, one May day in 2005, she had a major seizure. "Our life changed overnight,"[19] says Lisa. She began having seizures several times every day. Eventually, she lost the ability to walk and talk and had to be fed through a feeding tube in her stomach.

Niemann-Pick disease affects how the body metabolizes fatty substances called lipids, such as cholesterol. High levels of cholesterol build up in the brain, which causes damage to the brain tissue. Symptoms usually begin to show in young school-age kids, like Jessica. In addition to seizures, they may develop trouble with learning and memory, and Niemann-Pick

An accumulation of fat cells in the liver, spleen, bone marrow, and brain is characteristic of Niemann-Pick disease, which affects young children and results in various symptoms, including dementia.

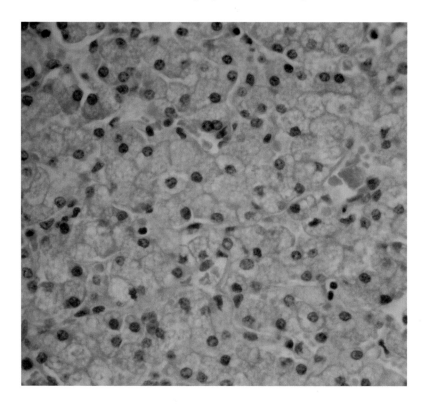

has been called the children's version of Alzheimer's disease. Eventually, affected children lose the ability to walk, communicate with words, and swallow food and fluids. There is no treatment for Niemann-Pick disease, and children with it rarely live past their teens.

Another type of dementia seen in children is Batten disease. Batten disease is a genetic disease that is caused by a buildup of substances, called lipopigments, in many body tissues, including the brain, muscles, eyes, and skin. It causes changes in personality and behavior, uncoordinated movements, vision problems, and slow learning. As the disease gets worse, symptoms of dementia worsen, and the child may have seizures or muscle spasms and lose his ability to walk and feed himself. Eventually, he becomes blind, unable to move or communicate, and is completely dependent on others for his care. As with Niemann-Pick, children with Batten disease rarely live through their teens.

## Other Causes of Dementia

There are many other disorders that can cause dementia or include symptoms of dementia. Many of them are genetic and run in families or occur mostly in certain parts of the world. Some illnesses of other body systems can also cause dementia symptoms, such as diseases of the thyroid, liver, lungs, pancreas, or kidneys. People with type 2 diabetes, a disease of sugar metabolism, are at a much higher risk for dementia. Brain infections, tumors, and head injuries can all cause dementia symptoms that may or may not be reversible, depending on the cause and severity. The long-term abuse of alcohol and illegal drugs, as well as exposure to toxic chemicals (especially lead) can damage the brain and cause irreversible dementia. Even nutritional deficiencies, especially of vitamin B, can cause dementia symptoms if they are not treated.

# CHAPTER THREE

# Diagnosis and Treatment

The large number of causes of dementia, as well as the similarity of the symptoms from one cause to another, can make diagnosis and treatment of dementia very difficult. Sometimes the diagnosis is made only after the person has died, and the brain tissue is examined during an autopsy. With all kinds of dementia, however, early diagnosis is very important, for several reasons. It may be that the person's symptoms are caused by something that is treatable, in which case they may be reversible. Even if the cause is found to be something that is irreversible, prompt treatment of the symptoms can help slow their progression. Early diagnosis of an irreversible disease also gives the person the chance to manage his symptoms better and help plan for his future while he is still able to think clearly and make decisions about his own care. Because early diagnosis is so critical, it is very important for the person with early dementia symptoms to seek medical care as soon as possible.

## Seeking Medical Care

For a number of reasons, people with dementia symptoms sometimes delay seeking medical care. They and their families may be unwilling to think about the possibility that they could be facing this kind of disease, with a rather grim future ahead. Dr. Eric Tangalos of the Mayo Clinic says, "There remains a tremendous anxiety regarding Alzheimer's. They want to blame

People with dementia symptoms and their families are often reluctant to pursue medical care out of fear or denial, knowing that an official diagnosis brings the certainty of a long, slow decline.

aging even when they can tell that other people their age aren't having the same difficulties. People hide their symptoms, or spouses cover for them. There's a fear of losing control. They don't want to give up their driving privileges or go in a nursing home."[20] Cary, a man with Alzheimer's, describes how he feels, "When I make a blunder, I tend to get defensive about it. I have a sense of shame for not knowing what I should have known. And for not being able to think things and see things that I saw several years ago, when I was a 'normal' person. But everybody, by this time, knows that I'm not a normal person. And I'm quite aware of that."[21]

Sometimes doctors themselves are reluctant to make a diagnosis of dementia. "Many doctors still believe that an early diagnosis of Alzheimer's would overwhelm both families and physicians," says Dr. Tangalos, but he stresses the importance of early diagnosis and treatment. "I don't want my patients or families to hide from it. We think there is a lot that can be done for the problem and that the sooner it is recognized, the more we have available as treatment options. It's a real disease, long before it prevents a person from functioning, and we need to do something about it."[22]

The first step in diagnosis usually happens when friends or family members notice that something is different about the person. They notice that his personality and behavior have changed, or that he forgets where he is or who family members are, or that his forgetfulness is interfering with his ability to take care of himself. The person himself may not even be aware that there is a problem until others bring it up. These changes lead the person to make the decision to visit his doctor.

## History and Physical Examination

Because early diagnosis of dementia symptoms is so important to starting the right treatment, the doctor will first conduct a complete health examination. He will do a detailed interview with both the patient and those close to him, in order to get a thorough and accurate picture of the kinds of symptoms the person has been having. He will ask about the patient's medical history, including any long-term health issues the patient may have, any injuries or surgeries he has had (especially those involving the head), and the medications he is currently taking. If the person is taking a lot of medications, he may have the patient stop taking some of them, to make sure the dementia symptoms are not caused by the medications interacting with each other in harmful ways.

Along with the medical history, a thorough physical examination is done. The physical examination helps make sure that the symptoms are not caused by some treatable condition, such as thyroid disease, kidney failure, or nutritional deficiencies. The doctor may order tests of blood and urine to help find any of these problems. The doctor will look for weakness on one side of the body or other signs that the person may have had a stroke.

## Specialists

After the interview and the physical exam, if the doctor suspects that the person is developing some type of dementia, he may send the patient to see a specialist, a doctor who focuses on one aspect of health care. For example, a gerontologist

---

# Franz Nissl

Franz Nissl (1860—1919) was a German neurophysicist who was very interested in diseases that affect the neurons in the cerebral cortex. He is best known for developing a special blue stain, now called Nissl's stain, which helps identify both normal and abnormal structures in the neurons. He used the stain to identify a protein-like substance unique to neurons, which came to be called Nissl's substance.

Nissl's father, who taught Latin in a Catholic school, wanted Franz to become a priest, but he defied his father and went to medical school at the University of Munich instead. He invented his staining technique while he was still a student, as part of a competition for a prize in neurology offered by the professors. The professors were so impressed with Nissl's work that they awarded the prize to him.

After completing medical school, Nissl worked in several positions, studying and writing about mental and neurological diseases. In 1889 he went to Frankfurt, where he met Alois Alzheimer. They became very good friends and worked together for seven years. After that, Nissl moved to the University of Heidelberg, where he eventually became head of the Department of Psychiatry. Unfortunately, severe kidney disease prevented him from finishing much of his research, and he died in 1919 at the relatively young age of fifty-nine.

Outside of his work, Nissl was a music lover and a gifted pianist. He is said to have had a sharp sense of humor and liked to play jokes on his professors.

specializes in the health problems of the elderly. A neurologist specializes in disorders of the nervous system. He may also suggest that the patient visit a psychiatrist or psychologist, just to make sure that the symptoms are not caused by a psychological problem such as anxiety or depression, which is fairly common in older people. A fourth specialist that may be involved is a neuropsychologist, who studies the relationship between brain functions and behavior, and can determine the level of impairment caused by brain disorders, stroke, or head injuries.

## The Neuropsychological Examination

If the patient is sent to a specialist, more specific tests, called neuropsychological tests, are done. Dr. Eric Tangalos explains what they do:

> These are mental tests that look at different functions in the brain. Different parts of the brain do different things. Language can be affected, or problem-solving. These tests break down the function of the brain into more basic

A doctor administers one of many types of tests that are conducted on patients with symptoms of dementia. By assessing the patient's overall performance on the various aspects of a neuropsychological exam, doctors can pinpoint the problem or disease behind the symptoms.

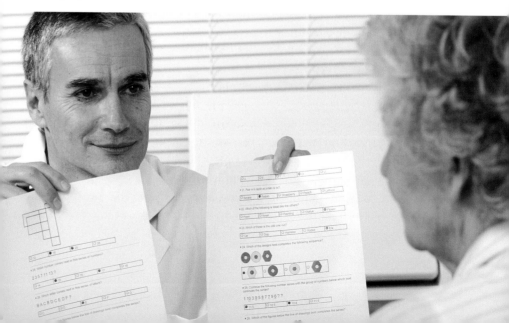

elements. Short-term memory is different from long-term memory. Performing calculations is different from remembering words. Drawing pictures is different from working through a maze.[23]

The doctor giving this kind of test will test the patient's balance, coordination, reflexes, and his vision and hearing. The doctor will also measure mental functioning by testing the patient's memory, language skills, problem-solving skills, and his ability to do common everyday tasks such as tying shoes. Problems in particular areas can help pinpoint more precisely what the underlying problem might be. For example, if the patient has trouble with memory and doing simple tasks, the doctor may start to suspect Alzheimer's disease. Problems with language may cause him to suspect a stroke or brain tumor. Personality changes might suggest frontotemporal dementia.

## The Mini-Mental State Examination

One test that is commonly used early in the diagnostic process to measure cognitive ability in older adults is the Mini-Mental State Examination, or MMSE. This eleven-question test takes only about ten minutes to do and examines skills such as memory, attention span, language skills, and orientation (knowing the day, time, and place), as well as the person's ability to copy a shape on paper, write a sentence, and follow written and verbal directions. For example, to test orientation, the examiner may ask the person what day it is, what year it is, or what state and country he lives in. To test memory, he may ask the person to repeat three words, such as *apple*, *hat*, and *book*, and then ask him to say them again later in the testing process. The highest score is thirty points. A score of twenty-four to thirty is considered normal, twenty to twenty-three indicates mild cognitive difficulty, ten to nineteen indicates moderate dementia, and below ten indicates severe dementia. The test can also be used several times with the same patient to measure changes over time.

The MMSE does have some limitations. Because the test relies so much on a person's ability to see, hear, and write, the results of the test can be affected if the person, for some reason, is unable to hear the directions well, see the paper, or understand English. He may not be able to draw or write well because of difficulty holding or using a pencil. The examiner takes these things into account when scoring the test. Also, highly educated people tend to score higher, even if they have Alzheimer's disease. The MMSE is never used to diagnose dementia all by itself; it must be used along with other diagnostic tests.

## Brain Scans

To get a more complete idea of what is actually going on in the brain, doctors may use brain scans. Brain scans are highly

A magnetic resonance imaging (MRI) scan of the brain of an Alzheimer's disease patient, right, shows a considerable loss of volume compared to a scan of a healthy brain, left. An MRI is one of several types of brain scan options available to doctors in helping them diagnose dementia symptoms.

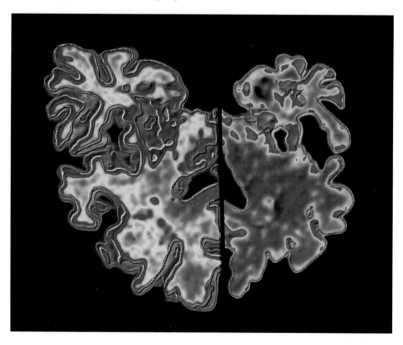

advanced techniques for getting a picture of the anatomy and function of the brain. They are similar to X-rays, except that they give a much more detailed image of the deeper structures in the brain. Brain scans show abnormalities in the size and shape of the parts of the brain and help doctors to pinpoint specific problems that may be the cause of dementia symptoms. Brain scans can find problems such as bleeding into the brain or brain tumors. They can also show cortical atrophy—degeneration and shrinking of the cortex—which is common in many types of dementia.

There are two basic kinds of imaging techniques. Structural imaging provides information about the shape and size of the brain and its parts. The two most common kinds of functional imaging methods are computed tomography scans (CTs) and magnetic resonance images (MRIs). CTs use X-rays to provide a three-dimensional picture of the brain and its structures. They can show brain atrophy, damage caused by strokes, tumors, bleeding, and changes in the blood vessels in the brain. An MRI is similar to a CT except that it uses a magnetic field and radio waves, instead of X-rays, to create the picture. It can detect the same problems as a CT but is somewhat better at showing brain atrophy and damage from very small strokes.

One very valuable advantage of an MRI is that doctors can use it to diagnose patients afflicted with Alzheimer's disease and those with vascular dementia. "Being able to determine that there is a vascular component to a patient's dementia would make a big difference in planning for treatment," says Dr. Norbert Schuff of the San Francisco VA Medical Center. "If we can tell the difference between people with Alzheimer's and those with vascular dementia, we can select the appropriate candidates for clinical trials of new drugs."[24]

## PET Scans

The other kind of imaging technique is called functional imaging. Functional imaging shows not only how the brain looks but also how well the brain cells are working by measuring functions like sugar metabolism, blood flow, and oxygen use.

Knowing how the brain's cells are functioning chemically helps doctors learn how well the brain as a whole is working. One very highly advanced and specialized kind of functional scan, developed in the 1950s, is called positron emission tomography, or PET. PET scans can pick up abnormalities in the brain even if the CT or MRI appears normal.

PET scans use very small amounts of radioactive substances called radiotracers. The radiotracers can be injected into a vein, taken by mouth, or inhaled as a gas. In the body, they give off energy in the form of gamma rays. The gamma rays are picked up by either a PET scanner, a special camera called a gamma camera, or a gamma probe. These devices work with a computer which turns the signals into a picture that shows how much of the radiotracers are absorbed by different organs

A positron emission tomography (PET) scan image of a healthy brain, left, is contrasted with a scan of the brain of an Alzheimer's patient. The red and yellow areas, which are prominent in the healthy brain, indicate a high level of brain activity; the blue and black areas, which dominate the Alzheimer's brain, show areas of low brain activity and indicate a reduction of function and blood flow.

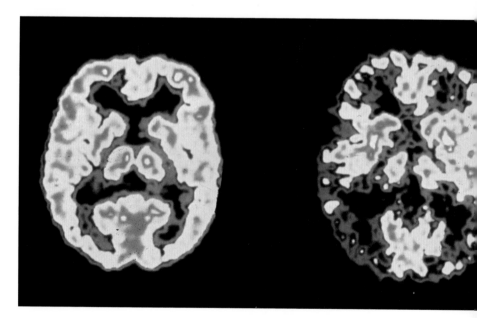

and tissues in the body. "Hot spots" on the image show where large amounts of the radiotracers are absorbed, indicating a lot of chemical activity. "Cold spots" show areas of smaller concentration and less chemical activity.

PET scans are commonly used to diagnose and treat cancers and heart diseases, but they are also useful for measuring brain function. They do it by measuring the amount of sugar metabolized by the brain. The less sugar metabolism, the less active that part of the brain is. PET scans are very good at detecting changes in the brain that are specific to different types of dementia. They can also detect the cause of those changes. For example, they have been shown to be extremely accurate in diagnosing Alzheimer's disease at a very early stage, and can even help predict if a person with mild memory problems will eventually develop dementia. "PET's ability to diagnose dementia in its earliest stages holds great significance," says Dr. Dan Silverman, professor of pharmacology at UCLA, "because medical management offers the most benefit during the initial period of decline. Physicians can also use the scans to reassure patients that their symptoms are not due to Alzheimer's or other diseases that cause mental decline."[25]

## Electroencephalograms

An electroencephalogram (EEG) is a test that measures and records electrical activity within the brain, and is used to help diagnose many types of brain problems. An EEG is done by placing electrodes on the skin over several parts of the brain. The electrodes pick up electrical activity from the brain and transfer the information to a machine that prints out the activity as a series of wavy lines on paper. The pattern of the lines indicates whether the electrical activity is normal or abnormal. Abnormal patterns of activity can indicate cognitive problems in specific parts of the brain or in the entire brain. EEGs can also detect seizures, which occur in about 10 percent of patients with Alzheimer's disease.

## Treating Dementia

A diagnosis of dementia can be devastating to a patient and his family, but it can also be seen as a positive thing. Kris, from Georgia, remembers how she responded to her early diagnosis at age forty-six: "I sought medical attention and after eight long months of testing . . . I was diagnosed with Alzheimer's disease. It was a relief to me because there was a name to it. Although it is an incurable disease, at least I knew what I was dealing with. All of that was five years ago, and thanks to the available medicine in the marketplace, I am able to live a somewhat normal life."[26]

Once a diagnosis is made, or even if it is simply suspected but not confirmed, treatment can begin. For reversible types of dementia, such as those caused by infections, hormone imbalances, or nutritional deficiencies, the goal of treatment is to

# When Is Forgetfulness Not Dementia?

Almost everyone has occasionally forgotten where they put something, or the name of the movie they saw just last week. Older people jokingly will say they are having a "senior moment." This kind of forgetfulness is common, especially in people over forty, and it tends to become more frequent as we age. But where do doctors draw the line between this normal forgetfulness and a serious problem like Alzheimer's disease?

Over the last decade, researchers have looked more closely at this kind of memory loss to try to determine if it is normal, or an indicator of worse problems to come. They now feel that some memory loss is not necessarily a predictor of dementia. They call it mild cognitive impairment (MCI) or cognitive impairment, not dementia (CIND). MCI has two forms. Amnestic MCI involves mostly memory loss (*amnesia* is the medical term for memory loss). Nonamnestic MCI involves other cognitive correct the cause, reverse the symptoms as much as possible, and help the patient return to a more normal life. Even if the dementia is irreversible, there are still things that can be done to help manage or even slow down the worsening of the symptoms, improve the patient's quality of life, and help the patient and his family cope with the disease.

## Managing Medications

Many elderly people need medications for health problems such heart disease, diabetes, high blood pressure, and kidney disease, among others. Sometimes these medications, especially when used in combination with lots of others, can interact with each other or have side effects that can cause dementia symptoms. One of the first steps for the doctor is to review all the medications the patient is taking, making sure that they are

impairments, such as language, concentration, reading, or writing problems.

To make a diagnosis, doctors conduct several neurological tests, including a psychological evaluation, but the major factor doctors look at is how much the memory loss is interfering with the person's ability to carry out his activities of daily living. They talk to the patient and his family to see how much help he needs with things like managing his finances or providing for his own basic needs of food, clothing, shelter, and personal hygiene. If the person is still able to function independently, he is considered to have MCI. If the person cannot perform the activities because of the memory loss, then it is most likely dementia, and further tests are done to confirm the diagnosis.

Currently, there is no sure way to predict whether or not a person with MCI will go on to develop dementia, although some studies have suggested that those with amnestic MCI are at higher risk for developing Alzheimer's disease. There is no specific treatment for MCI, although studies are looking at how well treatments for Alzheimer's might work.

really necessary, that the dosages are correct, that the patient is taking them correctly, and that they are not causing side effects or interacting with each other.

## Medications for Dementia

When the doctor is confident that the drugs the patient is already taking are being managed correctly, he may consider adding medication for the dementia itself. Many different kinds of medications are used to help treat dementias. To date, there is no medication of any kind that can cure dementia, although some medications can sometimes slow the symptoms of certain dementias in their early stages. For people with vascular dementia, for example, the doctor may prescribe drugs that control blood pressure and cholesterol, to help prevent strokes and further damage to blood vessels. Careful treatment of vascular dementia can help stop the symptoms from worsening.

So far, the medications that seem to work the best for dementias like Alzheimer's disease or Lewy body disease are drugs

Drugs like Aricept, a cholinesterase inhibitor that prevents the breakdown of acetylcholine, a key brain chemical, help to ease the symptoms and slow the progression of dementia in some patients.

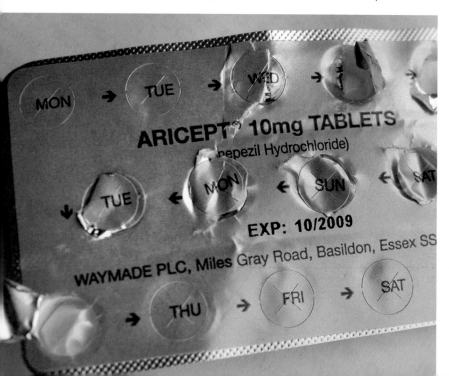

called cholinesterase inhibitors. Cholinesterase is an enzyme, naturally made in the body, which breaks down another chemical called acetylcholine. Acetylcholine is a very important chemical in the brain, especially in the cerebral cortex and the hippocampus. It is one of a group of chemicals called neurotransmitters that allow neurons to transmit messages to each other. Acetylcholine is involved with attention and wakefulness, among other nervous system functions.

People with Alzheimer's have a lower level of acetylcholine in their brains. Cholinesterase inhibitors prevent cholinesterase from breaking down acetylcholine. By interfering with the action of cholinesterase, more acetylcholine is available to the brain and brain function is improved. Cognitive functions such as memory and learning improve, and there is some evidence from research that behavior and personality can also improve.

Cholinesterase inhibitors do not work for everyone with dementia, and even when they do, the effect is not very great. They cannot stop the symptoms—they can only slow them down for a while. Also, the effects are only temporary because they cannot change the condition that caused the dementia in the first place. They can have unpleasant side effects such as sleep problems, muscle cramps, nausea, diarrhea, loss of appetite, and weight loss.

Another kind of drug that has been shown to be helpful even in the later stages of Alzheimer's is memantine. Memantine works in an entirely different way than cholinesterase inhibitors. It works with another neurotransmitter called glutamate. Glutamate is the most common and one of the fastest-working neurotransmitters in the brain and is involved with learning and memory. It is thought that, in Alzheimer's disease, there is a malfunction in the way glutamate does its job. Memantine helps to normalize the way glutamate transmits messages between neurons and helps improve the brain's ability to learn and remember.

Like the cholinesterase inhibitors, memantine cannot cure or reverse dementia, but treatment seems to be more effective when the patient takes both kinds of drugs together. Memantine can also have some side effects, such as dizziness, sleepiness, high blood pressure, headache, constipation, confusion, hallucinations, and sleep problems.

## Dietary Supplements

Nondrug treatment methods that many people try are dietary supplements. In recent years, a variety of vitamins, herbal extracts, and other supplements have been advertised as memory enhancers or treatments for dementia. These products have not been approved by the Food and Drug Administration (FDA) for dementia treatment and have not been put through the demanding process of research and testing that approved medications go through. Their effectiveness is not measured, and any bad side effects they may have do not have to be reported. They may contain ingredients that are not listed on the label, and they may interfere with the action of other medications. Some dietary supplements, however, such as ginkgo biloba and fish oil, may provide some benefit for dementia patients, and their effects are being researched.

If nondrug methods do not work adequately, then medications may have to be added. Medications to treat behavior are used very carefully in adults with dementia, starting with low doses, because they are more prone to experience severe side effects. There are no drugs available that are specifically approved by the FDA to treat the behavioral symptoms of dementia, but some kinds of drugs originally created to treat other conditions may be helpful in some people. Antidepressants can improve mood and decrease irritability. Antipsychotic drugs help control hallucinations and delusions and help decrease aggression and hostility. Anxiolytics are drugs that reduce anxiety and restlessness and help the person feel calmer.

## Treating Behavioral Symptoms

Many people with dementia behave in ways that they never would have before they became ill. They may have emotional outbursts of anger, hostility, or aggression or begin to cry for no apparent reason. They may engage in compulsive behavior, such as shredding paper or pacing back and forth. These behaviors can be triggered by a number of things, such as a disruption in routine, being hospitalized, getting a new caregiver, or having hallucinations or delusions.

Behavioral problems can be treated in several ways, either with medications or with nondrug approaches. Methods that do not involve drugs are usually tried first. Some of the causes of behavior problems can be corrected, such as maintaining routine as much as possible, correcting problems with vision or hearing that might cause confusion, and making sure the person is not uncomfortable or in pain.

As yet, there is no cure for most dementias, and treatment methods are very limited in their effectiveness. One of the greatest challenges for the patient and his family, therefore, is to learn how to cope effectively with these illnesses.

# CHAPTER FOUR

# Living with Dementia

**D**ementia can be an extremely difficult condition to live with, both for the person who has it and the people who care about him. It is very difficult to watch a loved one who has always been healthy, active, and independent become totally dependent upon others for his or her care. Jan, the wife of a doctor who developed Alzheimer's disease in his fifties, describes what it is like for her: "It's difficult," she says. "It's really sad watching your best friend and the person you've been closest to just disappear. I suppose that's the hardest thing—watching him every day just go, so that now he's nothing like the man I knew. He's like a stranger. He's totally dependent."[27]

Adult children of parents with dementia often find their roles reversed; their parent, who took care of them for so many years, may now rely on them for total care, including feeding, dressing, bathing, and personal hygiene. Even young children and teens may find themselves in a caregiver role if a parent develops early onset dementia. Lindsey was eight when her father was diagnosed with Alzheimer's at age fifty-one. "We had to do everything," she says. "Get him in the shower, get him dressed, cook his meals and get his seat belt on in the car. It's really hard but we had to do it 'cause he's our family."[28] It takes a lot of understanding and patience to care for an adult who may have significant behavioral problems and may have no memory of the people who have been so important to him his whole life. Fortunately, there are many things that can be done to optimize quality of life for the person with dementia.

## Maintaining Independence

Many people in the earlier stages of dementia are still able to live independently in their own home. If the person does not have a spouse or other family member living with him, frequent checks by a neighbor or family member can allow the person to keep his independence without needing constant supervision. A visiting nurse or home health aide who makes regular visits to the home can help make sure the person is managing adequately and is taking his medications properly. He or she

# Assistive Technology

*Assistive technology* is a term that describes any device that is specifically designed to promote independence and make life easier for the person with dementia and his caregivers. Assistive devices can be simple, like magnifying glasses, hearing aids, pillboxes, or canes, or they can be quite sophisticated, such as voice recognition software for the computer. According to the Family Caregiver Alliance, over 15 million Americans use some kind of assistive technology.

There are assistive devices for almost every aspect of daily living. For the kitchen there are gripping devices, easy-to-hold silverware, jar openers, and specially designed dishes, cutting boards, and utensils. For the bedroom and bath there are a multitude of devices for convenience and safety, such as grip bars, bed rails, tub mats, night-lights, raised toilet seats, and markers for hot and cold water, among many others. Aids to help with grooming and hygiene include specially designed clothing, no-rinse shampoos and body washes, bath seats, and nontie shoelaces. Devices to help people get around include canes, walkers, power wheelchairs, and lift vests that help caregivers lift and move the person. For those who have trouble communicating, modified telephones with large buttons, speakerphones, and voice recognition computer software help people keep in contact.

can also watch for new problems and issues that arise and help develop a plan for dealing with them.

It is important for the person living at home to feel safe and comfortable. Preventing falls and accidents is especially important. Some minor adaptations to the home, appropriate for the stage of the person's dementia, can help keep him safe. Grab bars and rubber mats in the bathroom help prevent slips in the shower or bathtub, and lowering the hot water temperature helps prevent scald burns. Even with these precautions, however, the person with dementia should never be unattended while bathing. Small area rugs and exposed electrical extension cords can cause falls and should be removed. Dangerous objects such as household chemicals, kitchen knives, and tools can be placed out of reach, locked up, or removed. Knobs on the stove can be removed or covered to help prevent burns and fires, and appliances that produce heat, such as coffeemakers or toasters, can be unplugged when not in use.

## Driving

Safety considerations also apply to activities outside the home, particularly driving. Living independently usually includes the ability to get in a car and drive, but driving can be hazardous for the person with dementia, as well as for other drivers on the road. A 2008 study conducted by Brown University and Rhode Island Hospital showed that people with even mild dementia had more accidents and did worse in road tests than those without any dementia. "Our findings showed that people with mild dementia were almost four times more likely to fail a road test than those with very mild dementia, indicating that people with very mild dementia may be able to drive safely for longer periods of time," says Dr. Brian Ott, lead researcher of the study. "It is clear, however, that driving ability declines fairly rapidly among patients with dementia, and therefore, regular follow-up assessments are warranted in these people with very mild dementia."[29] *Risk of Driving and Alzheimer's Disease*, clinical practice guidelines published by the American Academy of Neurology, recommends that people with very early dementia who want to drive should have their driving skills professionally tested every six months.

Eventually, all people with irreversible forms of dementia will have to give up driving because of the progressive nature of the disease. It can be difficult for the person and his family to make the decision about when he should stop driving. Family members can watch for signs that driving is no longer safe, such as loss of coordination, troublemaking decisions, getting lost, inability to do several tasks at once, and inability to pay attention to his surroundings. The most important issue is safety. If the person forgets that he should not be driving, or if he insists on driving after it has become unsafe, it may be necessary for the family to restrict his access to a vehicle by taking his keys or moving the vehicle to another location.

## Physical Health

Maintaining the best possible physical health helps the person with dementia remain independent and enjoy life as much as possible. Regular aerobic exercise, even just a daily walk around the block or a short swim at a fitness center, increases blood flow to the brain, lowers blood pressure, strengthens the

An elderly man uses a pulley exerciser at his retirement home in an effort to maintain his physical fitness. Regular exercise, combined with a healthful diet, can help senior citizens avoid or stave off the effects of dementia.

heart and lungs, controls weight, helps minimize restlessness and boredom, and helps relieve stress and depression. Exercise with weights helps maintain muscle mass and increases strength and metabolism to help control weight and blood sugar. Exercises that promote balance and flexibility, such as yoga or tai chi, help the person avoid falls and injuries.

A healthy diet, low in fat and calories and high in protein, helps maintain a healthy weight and helps control other conditions the person may have, such as diabetes, high blood pressure, or heart disease. Some people with moderate or late dementia may actually forget to eat, so caregivers must make sure the person is well nourished and drinks enough liquids. The person may need to have his meals prepared for him, with food cut up or finger foods provided to make it easier to eat. If the person has poorly fitting dentures or other trouble chewing or swallowing, the food may need to be chopped more finely or even pureed in a blender. Covered cups can help the person drink fluids more easily. Those in the advanced stages of dementia may need to be fed by another person. For those who can no longer swallow safely, a feeding tube may need to be surgically placed in their stomach or intestine in order to get the nutrition they need.

## Maintaining Mental Health

Just as exercise and diet help promote physical health, there are things that can be done to help preserve mental health for the person with dementia. It is important for the person to maintain his social contacts as long as possible. Being out of the house with other people who know him and share his interests helps prevent feelings of isolation and loneliness. Participating in favorite activities, such as dancing, eating out, or going to plays helps keep the mind active and wards off boredom and depression. Many senior centers or other community centers offer organized events such as dances or socials that people with dementia can enjoy. At home, simple activities that exercise the brain, such as simple crafts, reading, jigsaw puzzles, card games, and paper-and-pencil games like crosswords help keep the mind sharp and focused.

Another important way to maintain mental health is to keep a regular daily routine. "People do better when they have a routine," says Dr. Eric Tangalos. "It allows them to refresh and reinforce their pattern of behavior every day. They get to relearn their habits over and over and this is good." Sudden changes in routine, especially in the intermediate stages of dementia, can cause real problems. Tangalos says,

> When you put them in strange surroundings, they don't do well. A change in routine is not good for people with Alzheimer's—there are just too many problems to try and solve. This change of routine is one of the reasons why people with Alzheimer's often have such a swift downturn after the death of a spouse. The spouse may have been helping to both think for and protect the person.[30]

## Sleep Changes

Adequate sleep is also very important to a person's overall physical and mental health. Many people with dementia experience sleep disturbances that can interfere with daily life. Doctors are not sure why this is, but they think that the changes in the brain caused by some dementias also affect the parts of the brain that regulate sleep and wakefulness. Some people may have trouble falling asleep or staying asleep. Others may have disruptions of normal sleep patterns—sleeping more in the daytime and less at night. Some may completely reverse these patterns and sleep all day and be awake all night.

Many people with dementia become more restless, agitated, and confused at the end of the day and into the night. Behavior becomes more difficult to deal with, and hallucinations and delusions can become more frequent. This is called "sundowning," and it is fairly common. It is thought that it is caused by a combination of exhaustion from the activity of the day, and by disruptions in the person's normal sleep cycle.

Sleep medications are generally not recommended for people with dementia unless the sleep disturbances are severe or the person's nighttime behavior is disruptive to others. They can cause confusion and increase the risk of falls, and they do not usually improve the quality of sleep for older people. Other nondrug methods to improve sleep and avoid sundowning include avoiding caffeine, alcohol, and smoking; maintaining regular times for going to bed and getting up; keeping the noise and activity level down in the house later in the day; and making sure the temperature is comfortable and the person is not having any pain at bedtime. A night-light can help avoid confusion and fear if the person wakes up during the night.

## Coping with Confusion and Disorientation

Confusion and disorientation are major symptoms of dementia and often occur with sundowning. Confusion means that a person cannot process the information he receives and interpret it correctly. He may be unable to pay attention to or understand what is going on around him. He may not be able to carry on a meaningful conversation, make decisions, or answer questions

Visual prompts such as lists, written directions, name tags, and calendars help a person with dementia better manage a daily routine.

properly. Disorientation means that a person has trouble with time, place, and person. For example, he may not know what day or month or even what year it is. He may not be able to say where he is, or he may forget his own name or who his family members are.

Confusion and disorientation can be extremely upsetting and can make life more difficult for both the person and his family. There are things that can be done, however, that are helpful. Sticking to a regular daily routine and keeping the environment simple, uncluttered, and quiet helps keep distractions down and helps the person to stay focused on what is going on around him. Caretakers can wear name tags and remind him frequently throughout the day of where he is, what day and time it is, and who they are. Calendars with large numbers also help him remember what day it is. Written directions help the person remember how to use appliances and, if they are still driving, how to get to where they are going.

# Wandering

Wandering is a common and potentially dangerous consequence of confusion and disorientation. It is estimated that as many as 50 to 70 percent of people with dementia wander and get lost at some time. Wandering is not a deliberate behavior; it is not like running away. The person who wanders most likely has a reason for it, but his reason may only exist because of his confusion. Others may not be able to know what the reason is because of his inability to communicate it to them. He may be looking for something or someone. He may think he needs to go to work or fulfill some other obligation from his past. If he has been moved out of his home, he may feel the need to return to it, or he may think he is lost and sets out to try to find a more familiar place. He may set out for a specific place and then forget where he is going and become lost. He may simply be bored, restless, or anxious and feel the need to walk.

Wandering can actually be life threatening, especially in areas where there is a lot of traffic, rough terrain, or extreme weather conditions. People with dementia cannot always tell when they are in a dangerous situation. They can easily become lost, and it can be very difficult to find them before they fall or become injured in some way. They often do not or cannot respond to others calling their name. Most wanderers, about 90 percent, are found within 1 mile (1.6km) of their home, usually walking along the road. If they are not found within twenty-four hours, as many as 50 percent of them may be found seriously injured or dead from exposure to weather, dehydration, lack of medications, or injuries.

There are precautions that caretakers can take to help prevent wandering behavior and to help return to safety the person who has wandered. Close supervision is important, but it is unrealistic to try to supervise an adult twenty-four hours a day. Doors can be fitted with new locks or with childproof

# The Safe Return Program

In 1993 the Alzheimer's Association developed the Safe Return Program. This program works with law enforcement and other emergency agencies to help return those who have wandered to their families. Families can register a loved one with dementia into a nationwide database that includes information about the person and his picture. If a person becomes lost, the program faxes the information to local law enforcement agencies to help them in their search. The local Alzheimer's Association chapter is also notified so that they can provide support to the family while the search is underway.

The Safe Return Program also provides identification materials for the person, such as bracelets, necklaces, wallet cards, and clothing labels. The materials have a toll-free telephone number that anyone can call if they find a lost person. The person's caregivers are then notified that he has been found and where he is. Since the program began it has helped return over eight thousand people to their homes.

Family members and rescuers celebrate the safe return of an 87-year-old man with Alzheimer's disease, second from right, who had spent the night in the woods with his dog after wandering away from his home.

doorknob covers, or with alarms that go off whenever the door is opened. The person should always wear some form of non-removable identification that lists his name, address, and telephone number, as well as any health issues he has. Neighbors should be aware of the person's tendency to wander, so that they can take him home if they see him out alone.

## Becoming a Caregiver

As the number of people with Alzheimer's disease and other dementias continues to rise, more and more people will find themselves providing at least part-time care to a parent or other relative. According to Stephen McConnell, vice president of public policy for the Alzheimer's Association, in 2007 nearly 10 million Americans over age eighteen provided 8.4 billion hours of care to loved ones with the disease, and that another 250,000 between eight and eighteen are providing care. Most caregivers are women, and most are over fifty years old.

Caring for a person with dementia is expensive, time-consuming, and very stressful, especially as the disease moves into the later stages and disability worsens. Caregivers must take

Counseling sessions that involve both the person with dementia and family members or caregivers can help everyone involved learn as much as possible about the details of the disease so that they can better manage their expectations and make future plans.

on the responsibility of handling everyday tasks like shopping for groceries, doing the laundry, cleaning the house, preparing meals, seeing to personal hygiene, paying bills, giving medications, and many others. They must also cope with the person's memory loss, difficult behaviors, and inability to communicate their needs. This all becomes even more stressful if the caregiver has her own family and career demands to see to.

An important first step for new caregivers is to get educated about the particular dementia that has been diagnosed. Knowing as much as possible about the disease helps caregivers know what to expect and how to prepare. It is much easier for the caregiver to be patient and helpful to the person when she understands why the person is behaving as he is. The entire family as well as close friends can be included in the education process, so that everyone understands what is happening and can contribute to planning for the future. Education can come from doctors, support groups, books, articles in magazines and journals, and information from organizations such as the Alzheimer's Association. There is a great deal of information about dementia on the Internet, but readers must take care that the site is a reputable one, sponsored by an organization with good credentials.

## Help for Caregivers

The person with dementia is not the only one who needs help. Caregivers sometimes tend to neglect their own physical and mental health for the sake of the person they are taking care of. Without help, overworked and overstressed caregivers can burn out and develop health problems of their own. According to a survey by the Alzheimer's Association, caregivers are at higher risk than others for developing health problems, such as high blood pressure, loss of appetite, fatigue, irritability, sleep problems, and anxiety, because of the emotional stress and physical demands of caring for an adult with dementia. Many also develop depression or abuse drugs or alcohol. According to the survey, caregivers see their doctors almost twice as much, take 71 percent more medications, and are hospitalized more frequently than others their age who are not caregivers. It is important for caregivers to ask for help and support when they need it and accept it when it is offered.

## Community Resources

One step that caregivers can take to help themselves and their loved one is to find out what resources and support services are available in their community. Community resources can provide financial advice and assistance, education, emotional support, and in-home help so that the main caregiver does not have to manage everything all by himself.

Resources such as Meals on Wheels, volunteer transportation services, and respite care provide relief for the caregiver who needs a break. Respite care services are places such as senior centers and adult day-care centers that provide meals, medications, and social activities for the person during the day so that the caregiver can go to work, take care of her own fam-

An activities coordinator, left, helps a dementia patient with an art project at a community respite program in Boise, Idaho. Such programs allow people with dementia to spend several hours in a safe, structured environment while giving their caregivers a chance to tend to other responsibilities or just take a break.

ily, pursue her own interests, or just rest. Some facilities also provide physical or occupational therapy to help maximize the person's abilities. Most also provide transportation to and from the facility. Respite care is also available as an in-home service, which has the advantage of allowing the person to stay in his familiar environment.

# Assisted Living Facilities

Assisted living facilities are communities where elderly people can maintain some level of independence and still get the help they may need with health care and activities of daily living such as preparing meals, bathing and dressing, and housekeeping. They are designed for people who cannot live completely independently, but do not need constant care. They are like a bridge between independent living and nursing homes. Most facilities create an individual plan of care for each resident based on his or her particular needs. The plan is updated as the resident's condition changes. Assisted living communities also offer opportunities for social contact and activities with other residents such as dances, parties, and bus trips.

Some assisted living facilities operate along with independent living residences and nursing homes. This kind of combination is called a continuing care retirement community, or CCRC. CCRCs can offer the full range of services from minimal or no help to total care. The resident can easily move from one area to another depending on how his needs change over time.

## Support Groups

Interaction with other adults who understand what caregiving is like provides emotional support, information, and advice for the caregiver. Support groups provide a safe place for the caregiver to talk about frustrations and concerns, without being judged. Together, the members of the group talk about the challenges they face every day and help each other find solutions. They can also help each other find additional community resources. Some support groups meet together in person. Others talk to each other on the telephone or communicate on the Internet. Another source of support comes from attending meetings and workshops offered by organizations that focus on dementia care, such as the Alzheimer's Association and the Family Caregiver Alliance.

## Making Difficult Decisions

For many caregivers, the burden of caring for their loved one with dementia eventually becomes too great as the disease progresses, and the symptoms become unmanageable. It may be that financial resources run out or that family relationships are being damaged because of the stress. Often, the most important issue is that the health of the primary caregiver, often an elderly spouse, has deteriorated to the point where they can no longer care for their loved one. Whatever the reason, families often must make the difficult decision to move their loved one from his home and place him in a nursing home.

A resident at a nursing facility for Alzheimer's patients gets a hug from the home's administrator. Families often struggle with feelings of guilt and uncertainty when making the decision to move a loved one with dementia to a nursing home.

The decision to place a loved one in a nursing home can be a very difficult one. Placement in a nursing home is sometimes seen as "giving up" on the person or abandoning him, and families may feel a lot of guilt with such a decision. The safety and welfare of the loved one and his caregiver are the most important things to consider. Other considerations are the location of the facility, the cost involved, the particular needs of the patient, opinions and recommendations from others, the overall quality and cleanliness of the environment, and the friendliness and caring attitude of the staff. It is important for the caregiver and the rest of the family to remember that even after their loved one is placed in a nursing home, they are still and will always be an important part of the person's life.

Living with dementia is difficult for everyone involved. But there can be some positive outcomes as well. Jan says that even though it has been very hard to watch her husband Jamie deteriorate, and even though her life has changed dramatically because of it, she has chosen to look on the bright side. "For us, our family's become much closer," she says. "My relationship with my mother has become just wonderful. Jamie's two brothers have become very close. I think it's changed, in lots of ways, the closeness of our friendship with them. So we've done lots of things together . . . as a family, and the children and I have talked about lots of relationships within the family. So that's been good."[31]

# CHAPTER FIVE

# The Future of Dementia

**B**ack in 1901, Dr. Alois Alzheimer had very little to offer his patient, Auguste D., when her husband brought her to his psychiatric hospital with severe symptoms of dementia. "All in all," he wrote in his presentation to his fellow doctors after her death, "we are faced obviously with a peculiar disease process."[32] In the more than one hundred years since he first described the disease that today bears his name, scientists and doctors have contributed an enormous amount of knowledge and understanding about dementia, its causes, diagnosis, and treatments, and even about the human brain itself. There is still much that remains a mystery, however, and many questions have yet to be answered, but researchers are making new discoveries at a very fast rate, and there is plenty of reason for hope and optimism for this devastating group of disorders.

## Learning More About the Brain

In 2003 scientists from around the world completed one of the most ambitious projects ever undertaken in the field of human biology. The Human Genome Project set out to identify every one of the approximately twenty-five thousand genes in human DNA—the microscopic chemical units that carry all the instructions for making all the different proteins that determine how a person looks, how his body and its organs work, and even how he behaves. The genome of any living organism is like a list of all the genes the organism has. The more complex the organism, the larger the genome.

In early 2008 an important discovery about the brain, made possible because of the Human Genome Project, was reported. Scientists at the University of California, Irvine discovered the gene that is thought to be responsible for the formation of the cerebral cortex. The gene, called Lhx2, is a "creator" gene—it tells brand-new cells called stem cells what kind of specialized cell they are to become. Lhx2 tells stem cells in the developing brain of an unborn baby to become the cerebral cortex. This discovery is exciting to scientists because it may soon be possible to use stem cells that have the Lhx2 gene to grow new neurons that can replace neurons in the brain that have been damaged from head injuries or diseases like Alzheimer's.

A geneticist uses a sequencing machine as part of his work with the Human Genome Project, which began as an effort to identify each of the genes found in human DNA in 2003. Genetic research has resulted in important discoveries about brain development and function.

# Workouts for the Brain

One of the important lessons learned from the Nun Study is that people who exercise their brains with mental activities are at a much lower risk of developing dementia. A 2006 study called the Advanced Cognitive Training for Independent and Vital Elderly Study (ACTIVE) looked at the benefits of structured cognitive training programs for older adults. The study showed that thinking skills such as memory, reasoning, and thinking speed were improved when the adults in the study participated in training sessions that involved games and activities designed to sharpen these skills. The study also found that the improvements lasted for several years, and that the sharpened skills helped the adults with everyday tasks such as grocery shopping, managing money, and reacting to road signs. "Beyond middle age," says one of the ACTIVE study researchers, "people worry about their mental sharpness getting rusty. This study offers hope that cognitive training may be useful."

"Mental Exercise Helps Maintain Some Seniors' Thinking Skills," *NIH News*, December 19, 2006, www.nih.gov/news/pr/dec2006/nia-19.htm.

A group of seniors use a software program containing games and tasks that help them exercise their brains.

In March 2008 another massive project was begun, again building upon the information learned about the human genome. Scientists at the Allen Institute for Brain Science in Seattle, Washington, began a new project with the goal of describing how human genes influence the various parts of the brain and affect its functioning. The end result will be like a three-dimensional map of the brain—an atlas showing which genes are most active in which parts of the brain. A brain map like this was created for the mouse brain in 2006, and the scientists involved in this project hope that mapping the human brain in this way will help shed light on what goes wrong at the genetic level in diseases such as cancer, autism, and dementias.

## Dementia and Prevention

A large body of research is being done on learning more about dementia itself, especially Alzheimer's disease, and ways to prevent it from happening. Doctors know that beta amyloid plaques and tangles of tau protein are seen in the brains of Alzheimer's patients, but they are not 100 percent sure yet if the plaques and tangles actually cause the disease, or if they are a result of another disease, or if it might be a little of both. Beta amyloid is naturally made in the body and eventually gets cleared from the brain. One theory is that in Alzheimer's patients, the beta amyloid builds up faster than it can get cleared out, and the excess protein is toxic to the brain.

One of the main problems is that, by the time the plaques can be seen with brain imaging techniques, the damage has already been done. Scientists are now trying to come up with medications, which they call "plaque busters," that will actually help prevent the damage from the very beginning. The medications are enzymes that can break down clumps of beta amyloid protein so that it can be eliminated from the brain. "We have a robust pipeline of new medications in development," says Dr. Sam Gandy of the Alzheimer's Disease Research Center at Mount Sinai Hospital in New York, "many which are aimed at the buildup of amyloid and are disease-modifying."[33] The hope is that these new kinds of medications might not only prevent damage to the brain's neurons, but will also stabilize the symptoms if they have already developed, or even reverse symptoms.

## Alzheimer's and Caffeine

Plaque busters are one way that scientists hope dementia can be prevented. Recent research suggests that caffeine, the chemical in coffee, tea, and soda that helps people feel more awake, may also provide some protection against Alzheimer's disease. "Caffeine is the most widely used psychoactive drug in the world," says Gary Arendash, one of the researchers. "We think it might protect against Alzheimer's."[34] One study, published in early 2008, may explain why. It has to do with the blood-brain barrier.

The blood-brain barrier is a kind of filter that protects the brain from toxic substances in the blood. It is known that high blood levels of cholesterol can damage the barrier and make

Caffeine, a chemical found in coffee, tea, and soda, has been identified by some researchers as protecting the brain against Alzheimer's disease.

it leak. This leaves the brain more vulnerable to damaging substances in the blood. "High levels of cholesterol are a risk factor for Alzheimer's disease, perhaps by compromising the protective nature of the blood-brain barrier,"[35] says Jonathan Geiger, one of the researchers. In the study, rabbits that were fed a high-cholesterol diet were given either plain water or the equivalent of one cup of coffee to drink each day. The rabbits that had the caffeine showed much less damage to their blood-brain barrier as they got older than the rabbits that got the plain water. "Caffeine is a safe and readily available drug and its ability to stabilize the blood-brain barrier means it could have an important part to play in therapies against neurological disorders,"[36] Geiger says.

## A Fishy Theory

Another potential protection against Alzheimer's comes from fish. There is some research evidence that suggests that omega-3 fatty acids, a substance found in fish oils, may help prevent Alzheimer's disease. A 2007 study from the University of California, Los Angeles (UCLA) showed that an omega-3 fatty acid called DHA increases the production of a protein called LR11. LR11 destroys the toxic beta amyloid protein that forms plaques in the brains of Alzheimer's patients. "We found that even low doses of DHA increased the levels of LR11 in rat neurons, and dietary DHA increased LR11 in the brains of rats or older mice that had been genetically altered to develop Alzheimer's disease,"[37] says Greg Cole, the lead researcher. He says that more research is needed to determine what the best dose of DHA is, but he recommends that adults eat more fatty fish such as cod and salmon, or take a supplement.

## Preventing Dementia with Vaccines

One of the most reliable ways to prevent getting a disease is with a medication called a vaccine. Vaccines work by a process called active immunization—after the vaccine is injected into the body, it stimulates the body's natural immune response to produce antibodies, which are particles of protein that attack and destroy the organism that causes the disease. Children in the United States routinely get vaccines for disease like measles, mumps, rubella, tetanus, hepatitis, and diphtheria. Protection provided by the vaccine usually lasts for the person's whole lifetime.

Scientists are working to develop a vaccine for Alzheimer's that could trigger the immune system to produce antibodies that would attack the beta amyloid protein that is thought to be the main culprit in Alzheimer's. A vaccine developed in the late 1990s looked promising, but human testing was stopped in 2002 when some patients developed an abnormal and life-threatening immune response that caused a severe inflammation of the brain. One newer approach involves passive immunization. The antibodies are grown in a laboratory and then injected. "This is a different way to grow antibodies," says Dr. John Morris of Washington University in St. Louis, Missouri. "We grow them in test tubes and give them to patients so the patient can then launch an immune response, but since the body is not generat-

A mouse's brain cells containing dark clumps of protein cells associated with Alzheimer's disease, left, are contrasted with brain cells from a similar mouse that was treated with an experimental vaccine. Researchers are working to develop and refine a vaccine that attacks the proteins that are thought to cause the disease.

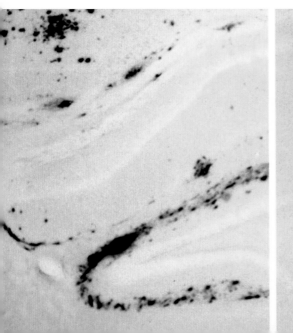

ing the antibodies on its own, they will not overstimulate their immune system."[38]

Other researchers are working with green monkeys to develop a more specific vaccine that can attack just the beta amyloid without having brain inflammation as a side effect. A group of scientists in Tokyo, Japan, are working on a vaccine that, instead of antibodies, uses a segment of DNA which carries the codes for making beta amyloid. The amyloid DNA stimulates the immune system more gently than regular vaccines. Still other researchers are working with mice to develop vaccines that can be inhaled as a nasal spray or applied to the skin as a cream or a patch. The vaccine gets absorbed into the bloodstream so the patient does not need an injection.

## Dementia and Blood Sugar

Another emerging theory about Alzheimer's disease is related to its connection to type 2 diabetes, a disease of sugar metabolism that is becoming increasingly common among older people, especially those who are overweight. All of the body's cells use glucose, a type of sugar, as a fuel source for carrying out their functions. The hormone insulin, made in the pancreas, makes it possible for the cells to use the glucose. In people with diabetes, however, their cells resist the action of insulin. Glucose builds up in the blood, which can cause lots of different health problems because the cells cannot get the fuel they need. This is especially important to the brain, because glucose is the only kind of fuel it can use.

If body cells become resistant to insulin, the body's natural response is to make more insulin. One theory about insulin and dementia is that excessive amounts of insulin in the blood may cause increased production of beta amyloid, which then builds up in the brain and forms plaques. Excess insulin may also interfere with the natural enzyme that breaks down beta amyloid, and this may be the reason that the amyloid does not get cleared out of the brain as it should.

A second theory is related to the fact that high blood sugar can damage blood vessels. Damage to the tiny vessels in the brain can cause symptoms of vascular dementia. Since vascular dementia and Alzheimer's often occur together, some scientists believe that the vascular damage may cause Alzheimer's symptoms to appear earlier.

Type 2 diabetes is thought to increase the risk of dementia by as much as 70 percent, and diabetics who control their blood sugar poorly have an even greater risk. If these theories about the connection between diabetes and dementia can be confirmed, it may mean that prevention and treatment methods for diabetes might also help some dementias.

## The Nun Study

In 1986 University of Kentucky scientist David Snowdon began one of the most comprehensive studies ever done of the human brain and Alzheimer's disease. He approached the nuns of the School Sisters of Notre Dame in Mankato, Minnesota, and asked them if they would let him study them to learn more about the aging process. He especially wanted to find out why some people get Alzheimer's disease and others never do. The nuns agreed to share details about their early lives and their families and to let him study their physical and mental health for the rest of their lives. They even agreed to give him their brains after their death to be dissected and examined.

Six hundred seventy-eight nuns have participated since the study began. The group is a good one to study from a scientific viewpoint because they are a homogenous group—they have all lived very similar lives, eating the same food, getting the same kind of health care, and doing the same kinds of activities. Almost all had been teachers. Scientific results are considered to be more accurate when the study group members are as similar to each other as possible.

Over the next two decades, the Nun Study, as it came to be called, revealed a great deal of information about the brain and Alzheimer's disease. Dr. Snowdon was able to confirm earlier research that suggested that the vitamin folic acid may help prevent Alzheimer's, that having a college education and staying physically and mentally active help protect a person from

Elderly nuns that belong to the School Sisters of Notre Dame
participated in a twenty-year study on the aging process that
resulted in many interesting discoveries about the brain and
Alzheimer's disease.

its effects, and that small strokes and head injuries may make
a person more likely to develop it. One surprising new finding, discovered by reading accounts of the nuns' lives written
when they first entered the convent, was that the way a person
expresses herself with language in early life can help determine
how long she'll live and her likelihood of developing Alzheimer's later in life. The nuns whose early writing expressed positive emotions and lots of different ideas, what Dr. Snowdon
calls "idea density," lived longer and had a much lower incidence of dementia than those whose writing was simpler and
less positive.

Dr. Snowdon knows that the Nun Study probably will not
lead to any new drugs or any new explanations about the
causes of dementia. Its value lies instead in discovering ways to
prevent the disease in the first place. It also demonstrates the

# The Eyes as Window to the Brain

A physician in Massachusetts with a background in ophthalmology, the study of diseases of the eye, has developed a theory that it may be possible to detect Alzheimer's disease in its very early stages with a simple eye examination. Dr. Lee Goldstein uses a type of laser to examine the lens of the eye to look for deposits of beta amyloid protein.

While studying mice that had been specially bred to develop Alzheimer's, he noticed that they had all developed a particular kind of cataract, or clouding of the lens, in their eyes. The cataract was different from the usual kind of cataract that older people often get, and regular mice did not have the cataracts in their eyes. Using a special kind of eye laser, he discovered that beta amyloid molecules had built up around the edge of the lens in the Alzheimer's mice. He could see this change even before the amyloid had begun to build up in their brains. Dr. Goldstein and his colleagues hope that this simple and painless test will help diagnose Alzheimer's at a very early stage, as well as keep track of the progression of the disease and evaluate the effectiveness of treatment methods.

close connection between a person's early life and their health in later life. "I think the Nun Study is very important because it uses information obtained about people before the period of illness," says Dr. Robert Friedland, an Alzheimer's researcher. "So we know from the Nun Study and others that Alzheimer's disease takes several decades to develop, and the disease has many important effects on all aspects of a person's life,"[39] Adds Dr. Snowdon, "We'll continue to learn from the sisters for many, many years to come."[40]

## Progress in Diagnosis

Learning more about dementia disorders themselves and how to prevent them is just one area of research that shows promise for the future. It is already known that early diagnosis is important for managing dementia more effectively. Scientists are working to find ways to diagnose dementias sooner and more accurately so that the right course of treatment can be started. Says Gary Small, director of the UCLA Center on Aging, "One of the most important strategies is early detection, because it's going to be easier to protect a healthy brain than try to repair one once the damage has been done."[41]

With earlier diagnosis as their goal, researchers are working on the development of new brain-scanning techniques that can identify the actual beta amyloid plaques and tao protein tangles that are involved in Alzheimer's disease. In these new methods, a chemical marker is injected into the patient. The marker travels into the brain and sticks to the plaques and tangles. Then a PET scan is done. The areas of the brain that have the most marker in them show where the most plaques and tangles are.

Another similar technique is showing promise for early detection of frontotemporal dementia (FTD), a form of dementia that is frequently mistaken for Alzheimer's. In this technique, a radioactive form of glucose is injected and taken up by the brain. Areas of lower brain activity take up less of the radioactive sugar. In FTD, the front of the brain has less activity. In Alzheimer's, the back of the brain is less active. "Early diagnosis of FTD can have a tremendous impact on the treatment for patients and their family members," says Dr. Norman Foster, the leader of the study. "Many patients are misdiagnosed and may be hospitalized and receive drugs for the wrong disease."[42]

## Improvements in Treatment

Scientists are rapidly learning more about dementia and new ways to diagnose it earlier and more accurately. As valuable as early diagnosis is, however, there must be effective treatments to offer once the early diagnosis is made. Scientists are concentrating their efforts on finding treatment strategies that do more than just treat the symptoms. "We're at a juncture now where we're trying to make the transition from treating symptoms to disease-modifying treatments," says researcher Dr. Norman Relkin of New York Presbyterian Hospital. "A whole new window is opening in terms of the approach to the disease."[43] Most research is targeted toward developing medications that destroy beta amyloid plaques.

## Immunotherapy

In 2007 Dr. Relkin and his colleagues discovered naturally occurring antibodies in the blood that they believe may help to protect people against Alzheimer's and other diseases like it, such as Lewy body dementia. These antibodies attack the clusters of beta amyloid protein that make up the plaques of Alzheimer's, but do not attack harmless single pieces of beta amyloid. Dr. Relkin and his team have been testing a treatment method called immunotherapy, which uses these natural antibodies collected from the blood of healthy people. They call the treatment intravenous immunoglobulin (IVIG), and their results have been promising. "The effects of IVIG in lowering beta amyloid levels in Alzheimer's patients . . . were much more profound than we expected,"[44] says Dr. Relkin. IVIG seems to be able to tell the harmful plaques from the harmless single pieces by their shape, even though they are chemically the same. "This was a surprise," says coauthor of the study Dr. Paul Szabo, "because most antibodies work by recognizing some aspect of the chemical structure of their target—not their shape."[45]

## SALAs

Another class of drugs that have promise for targeting the buildup of amyloid plaques is called selective amyloid-beta lowering agents (SALAs). SALAs help lower the amount of beta amyloid protein in the brain by changing the way it is created. Beta amyloid is created when an enzyme called gamma secretase cuts up longer pieces of protein, called APP, into fragments. SALAs work by making the gamma secretase cut up the APP into shorter, nontoxic pieces that do not clump together

A woman with Alzheimer's disease, right, posing with her daughter, is a participant in a trial for the experimental drug Flurizan, one of a class of drugs known as selective amyloid-beta lowering agents (SALAs) that have shown promise in slowing the decline of Alzheimer's patients.

the way beta amyloid pieces do. SALAs appear to work fairly well in the early stages of Alzheimer's, and early research on a SALA drug called Flurizan has shown that people with mild Alzheimer's did have slower rates of mental decline. Research is continuing to determine exactly how beneficial SALAs might be to Alzheimer's patients.

## A Challenging Future

As the elderly population continues to rise, and as medical advances make it possible for more and more people to live into advanced old age, the number of people with dementia will continue to rise dramatically. The stresses this will place on the health-care system and on those who must take care of all these people are enormous. The push is on to develop better ways to diagnose and treat dementias, and to provide meaningful training and resources for the millions of caregivers who give so much of themselves to care for their loved ones and keep them at home as long as possible. As one woman with vascular dementia says,

> What makes the best sense of all is empowering people with dementia to care for themselves as much as possible and for as long as possible. People with dementia absolutely can learn some things far into the disease. I truly believe that people with early dementia can be taught to better understand and manage their own disease and behaviors. I further believe that a society which allows people with dementia to stay involved in their chosen activities also prolongs life and emotional health.[46]

Research and discovery are proceeding at a fast pace, and doctors and scientists are optimistic for a much better future for dementia patients and their families. One researcher, Dr. Scott Small of Columbia University, is hopeful. "In the ten or twelve years that I've been involved in this," he says, "both in terms of seeing patients and in performing research, I've shifted from profound pessimism to cautious optimism."[47] With so much attention being given to learning about all aspects of dementia care, the future is looking brighter every day.

# Notes

## Introduction: The Memory Thief

1. Quoted in Jim Swyers, "Peculiar Material: Disbanding Unruly Mobs of Proteins," *Pittmed*, Spring 2007, p. 23.
2. Quoted in David Shenk, "The Memory Hole," *New York Times*, November 3, 2006, www.nytimes.com /2006/11/03/opinion/03shenk.html.
3. Shenk, "The Memory Hole."
4. Quoted in Kathleen Fackelman, "18% of All Boomers Expected to Develop Alzheimer's," *USA Today*, March 17, 2008, www.usatoday.com/news/health/2008-03-17-alzheimers-stats_N.htm.
5. Shenk, "The Memory Hole."

## Chapter 1: What Is Dementia?

6. Quoted in "Living with Dementia, Personal Stories," Alzheimer's Association, Minnesota–North Dakota Chapter, www.alzmndak.org/aboutus/whoweare/personalstories. Page accessed March 26, 2008.
7. Margaret O. Hyde and John F. Setaro, *When the Brain Dies First*. New York: Franklin Watts, 2000, p. 8.
8. Quoted in Daniel Kuhn, *Alzheimer's Early Stages*, 2nd ed. Alameda, CA: Hunter House, 2003, pp. 10–11.
9. Quoted in Susan Dentzer, "Sufferers of Early Onset Alzheimer's Describe Life with the Disease," transcript, *Online NewsHour*, January 10, 2008, www.pbs.org/newshour/bb/health/jan-june08/alzheimers_01-10.html.
10. Quoted in Steven Reinberg, "Two Parents with Alzheimer's Raises Child's Risk," *Health Day*, March 10, 2008, www.healthday.com/Article.asp?AID=6134158.

## Chapter 2: What Causes Dementia?

11. Kris, "Kris's Story," Alzheimer's Association, www.alz.org/
living_with_alzheimers_8810.asp.
12. Swyers, "Peculiar Material," p. 24.
13. Quoted in Story 4, *Lewy Body Journal*, August 28, 2007,
www.lewybodyjournal.org/stories/s16.html.
14. Quoted in Story 5, *Lewy Body Journal*, August 29, 2007,
www.lewybodyjournal.org/stories/s16.html.
15. Quoted in Thomas Goldsmith, "Aging Nation to Fight Dementia," *News & Observer*, April 5, 2006, www.news
observer.com/politics/politicians/helms/story/425440.html.
16. Quoted in Steven Reinberg, "High Blood Pressure
Linked to Disability, Dementia," *Health Day*, November 19, 2007, www.medicinenet.com/script/main/art.
asp?articlekey=85335.
17. Quoted in Goldsmith, "Aging Nation to Fight Dementia."
18. Quoted in Goldsmith, "Aging Nation to Fight Dementia."
19. Quoted in Kathleen Fackelman, "Alzheimer's Touches
Children," *USA Today*, May 1, 2006, www.usatoday.com/
news/health/2006-05-01-alzheimers-kids_x.htm.

## Chapter 3: Diagnosis and Treatment

20. Quoted in Mayo Clinic Staff, "Diagnosing Alzheimer's: An
Interview with a Mayo Clinic Specialist," MayoClinic.com,
December 5, 2006, www.mayoclinic.com/health/
alzheimers/AZ00017.
21. Quoted in "New Book Empowers People Living with
Dementia," *Medical News Today*, October 8, 2007, www.
medicalnewstoday.com/articles/84838.php.
22. Quoted in Mayo Clinic Staff, "Diagnosing Alzheimer's."
23. Quoted in Mayo Clinic Staff, "Diagnosing Alzheimer's."
24. Quoted in "Scans Spot Dementia Differences,"
*BBC News*, August 12, 2003, news.bbc.co.uk/2/hi/
health/3145285.stm.
25. Quoted in "Brain PET Scan Predicts if Memory Lapses
Will Progress Into Dementia, Detects Alzheimer's Disease
at Earliest Stages, UCLA-led Study Finds," *Science Daily*,
November 23, 2001, www.sciencedaily.com/
releases/2001/11/011120054932.htm.
26. Kris, "Kris's Story."

## Chapter 4: Living with Dementia

27. Jan, "Jan's Story," *Better Health Journal* (Victoria, Australia), www.betterhealth.vic.gov.au/BHCV2/bhcarticles
.nsf/pspages/ps_alzheimers_disease?open.
28. Quoted in "When Youth Is Shadowed by Alzheimer's,"
CBSNews.com, March 18, 2008, www.cbsnews.com/
stories/2008/03/18/eveningnews/main3949004.shtml.
29. Quoted in Robert Preidt, "Driving Skills Decline Among
People with Early Alzheimer's," *Health Day*,
January 24, 2008, www.healthday.com/Article.asp?
AID=611979.
30. Quoted in Mayo Clinic Staff, "Diagnosing Alzheimer's."
31. Jan, "Jan's Story."

## Chapter 5: The Future of Dementia

32. Quoted in "2006: The Year in Alzheimer's Science,"
Alzheimer's Association, 2006, www.alz.org/alzheimers_
disease-research-ad.asp.
33. Quoted in Betsy Noxon, "Breakthrough Discoveries,"
*MSN Health & Fitness*, http://health.msn.com/health-
topics/alzheimers-disease/articlepage.aspx?cp-docum
entid=100194627.
34. Quoted in Kathleen Fackelmann, "Can Caffeine Protect
Against Alzheimer's?" *USA Today*, November 5, 2006,
www.usatoday.com/news/health/2006-11-05-
caffeine-alzheimers_x.htm.
35. Quoted in Kevin McKeever, "Caffeine May Block High
Cholesterol Linked to Alzheimer's," *Health Day*, April 9,
2008, www.nlm.nih.gov/medlineplus/news/
fullstory_63223.html.
36. Quoted in McKeever, "Caffeine May Block High
Cholesterol."
37. Quoted in Madeline Vann, "Fish Oil May Help Prevent Alzheimer's," *Health Day*, December 28, 2007,
www.nlm.nih.gov/medlineplus/news/fullstory_59473.html.
38. Quoted in "A Vaccine for Alzheimer's?" Alzheimer's Disease Health Center, July 19, 2006, www.webmd.com/
alzheimers/news/20060719/vaccine-for-alzheimers.
39. Quoted in Pam Belluck, "Nuns Offer Clues to Alzheimer's

and Aging," *University of South Florida News*, May 7, 2001, www.stpt.usf.edu/~jsokolov/agealzh2.htm.
40. Quoted in "Nun Brains May Help Unlock Secrets of Alzheimer's," CNN.com, December 21, 2007, www.cnn.com/2007/HEALTH/12/21/nun.brains.ap/index.html.
41. Quoted in interview with Matt Lauer, *Today Show*, March 19, 2008. http://video.yourtotalhealth.ivillage.com/player/?id=230625&ice=th%7Cvid_tout%7C1.
42. Quoted in "PET Scan Distinguishes Alzheimer's from Other Dementia," University of Utah Health Sciences Center, November 1, 2007, www.eurekalert.org/pub_releases/2007-11/uouh-psd110107.php.
43. Quoted in Christine Larson, "Attacking Alzheimer's: The Latest News on Treatment and Diagnosis," *U.S. News & World Report*, January 31, 2008, http://health.usnews.com/articles/health/brain-and-behavior/2008/01/31/attacking-alzheimers.html.
44. Quoted in "Newly Discovered Antibody May Be Body's Natural Defense Against Alzheimer's," press release, New York Presbyterian Hospital/Columbia University Medical Center, June 11, 2007, www.eurekalert.org/pub_releases/2007-06/nyph-nda061107.php.
45. Quoted in "Newly Discovered Antibody."
46. Quoted in "Dreaming About a Cure, Talking About Care: Part 4 of 4," *The Tangled Neuron* Web site, www.tangledneuron.info/the_tangled_neuron/2006/12/dreaming_about__3.html.
47. Quoted in interview with Scott Bazell, *Today Show*, March 19, 2008. http://video.yourtotalhealth.ivillage.com/player/?id=230625&ice=th%7Cvid_tout%7C1.

# Glossary

**active immunization:** The immunity to disease that a person gets when he is exposed to a disease-causing organism and his body produces antibodies that protect the person from the disease.

**Alzheimer's disease:** The most common form of dementia, thought to be caused by abnormal protein deposits in the brain. Causes memory loss, impairment in cognitive function, and eventual helplessness.

**amyloid precursor protein (APP):** A protein molecule that, when cut by the enzyme gamma secretase, produces beta amyloid protein.

**antibodies:** Particles of protein that are made by the immune system and protect a person from disease.

**atrophy:** Shrinkage of an organ or body tissue from disease or lack of use.

**autopsy:** Examination of a body after death to determine the cause of death.

**axons:** Long threadlike projections that extend out from the body of a neuron that allow neurons to communicate with each other.

**Batten disease:** A form of brain disease seen in children that causes dementia in its later stages.

**beta amyloid:** Fragments of APP that collect into plaques in the neurons and destroy them, causing dementia.

**blood-brain barrier:** The natural barrier between the brain and the bloodstream that protects the brain from harmful substances in the blood.

**cerebral cortex:** The main part of the brain that controls consciousness, cognitive functions, and sensory input.

**cerebrum:** Another name for the cerebral cortex.

**cholesterol:** A fatty substance made naturally in the body and found in foods that can cause health problems if it builds up in the blood stream.

**cholinesterase:** An enzyme that breaks down the neurotransmitter acetylcholine.

**cholinesterase inhibitor:** A drug, commonly used to treat Alzheimer's disease, that inhibits the action of cholinesterase.

**cognitive:** Having to do with the higher brain functions of learning, memory, attention, and reasoning.

**computed tomography (CT) scan:** An advanced diagnostic technique that uses X-rays to provide a three-dimensional view of body structures.

**confusion:** A disorder of brain function in which a person is unable to process information correctly.

**corpus callosum:** A thick band of nerve tissue that connects the two hemispheres of the brain and allows them to communicate with each other.

**cortical:** Related to the cerebral cortex of the brain.

**declarative memory:** Memory for specific events and times in a person's life. Also called episodic memory.

**delusions:** Thoughts that a person believes to be true despite facts or proof that they are false.

**dementia:** A group of symptoms caused by brain malfunction that impair cognitive abilities.

**deterministic gene:** A gene that will cause disease even if only one is inherited.

**disorientation:** A disorder of brain function in which a person cannot tell what day, month, or year it is, who he is, who other people are, or where he is.

**electroencephalogram (EEG):** An examination of brain function in which electrodes are placed on the scalp and the electrical activity of the brain is measured and evaluated.

**encoding:** The first step of memory formation in which memories are stored.

**enzyme:** A chemical substance that can break down other chemicals. Names of enzymes often end in the suffix "ase," as in gamma secretase.

**episodic memory:** Memory for certain times and events in a person's life.

**frontal lobes:** The part of the brain located behind the forehead.

**frontotemporal dementia:** A form of dementia caused by damage in the frontal and temporal lobes of the cerebral cortex.

**gamma secretase:** The enzyme that cuts amyloid precursor protein into beta amyloid pieces.

**genome:** The entire list of genes for any living organism.

**gerontologist:** A doctor who specializes in the health issues of the elderly.

**gray matter:** The surface of the cerebral cortex, made of millions of neurons, and slightly gray in color.

**hallucinations:** Seeing things that are not there, or seeing something that is there and believing it is something else.

**hemispheres:** The two halves of the brain.

**hippocampus:** A part of the brain needed for making and storing memory.

**immunotherapy:** A treatment method that produces immunity to a disease or makes the immune system more resistant to a disease.

**Lewy body dementia:** A form of dementia similar to Alzheimer's disease, caused by abnormal protein deposits in the brain called Lewy bodies.

**lipopigments:** Substances that exist in the body's tissues, made up of fats (lipids) and proteins. The build-up of lipopigments to high levels causes Batten disease in children.

**lobes:** The four main sections of the brain.

**magnetic resonance image (MRI):** A scanning technique that uses a magnetic field and radio waves to provide a picture of the body's structures.

**multi-infarct dementia:** Another name for vascular dementia.

**neurofibrillary tangles:** Clumps of twisted threads of tau protein that are found in the neurons of the brains of Alzheimer's patients.

**neurologist:** A doctor who specializes in disorders of the nervous system.

**neuron:** A specialized cell of the nervous system that conducts messages using chemical and electrical impulses.

**neuropsychologist:** A doctor who specializes in the relationship between brain disorders and behavior.

**neurotransmitter:** A brain chemical that helps transmit messages between neurons.

**Niemann-Pick disease:** A form of dementia seen in children caused by abnormal metabolism of lipid such as cholesterol.

**nondeclarative memory:** Memory of knowledge, skills, and meaning of objects.

**occipital lobes:** The part of the brain located at the back of the head, mainly responsible for vision.

**organic brain syndrome:** An outdated term for dementia in the elderly.

**parietal lobes:** The section of the brain located at the top of the head, behind the frontal lobes.

**passive immunization:** A method of providing immunity to a disease by injecting antibodies that have been made in the laboratory.

**plaques:** Clumps of abnormal protein that collect between the neurons and cause their malfunction and death.

**positron emission tomography (PET):** An advanced scanning technique that can be used to study both structure (structural imaging) and function (functional imaging) of the body's organs.

**progressive nonfluent aphasia:** The inability to express oneself using language.

**radiotracers:** Radioactive chemicals used with PET scans to identify areas of activity in the brain.

**remote memory:** Memories of things that happened a long time ago.

**retrieval:** The ability to call a memory into consciousness when it is needed.

**risk genes:** Genes that, when inherited, increase a person's chances of developing a particular disease.

**semantic dementia:** A symptom of dementia in which words and phrases have no meaning to the person using them.

**senile dementia:** An outdated term for dementia in the elderly.

**short-term memory:** Memories for things that happened in the near past.

**stroke:** The sudden interruption of blood flow to a portion of the brain, causing symptoms such as weakness or paralysis on one side, slurred speech, and vision disturbances.

**subcortical:** Areas of the brain below the cerebral cortex.

**tau protein:** The protein that forms abnormal twisted threads, or tangles, in the brains of Alzheimer's patients.

**temporal lobes:** The part of the brain located on the sides of the head, behind the ears, responsible for emotions, hearing, language, and memory.

**vaccine:** A drug that stimulates the immune system to produce antibodies to a particular disease, making the person immune to the disease.

**vascular dementia:** A form of dementia caused by damage to or blockage of the small blood vessels in the brain.

**working memory:** A very short-term form of memory that stores small bits of information only as long as they are needed.

# Organizations to Contact

## Alzheimer's Association

225 North Michigan Avenue, 17th floor
Chicago, IL 60601
(800) 272-3900
www.alz.org
info@alz.org

The Alzheimer's Association, committed to finding a cure for Alzheimer's disease, has chapters in every state and provides education, research support, and support for patients and their caregivers.

## Alzheimer's Disease Education and Referral Center (ADEAR)

PO Box 8250
Silver Spring, MD 20907
(800) 438-4380
www.alzheimers.nia.nih.org
adear@alzheimer's.org

A service of the National Institute on Aging, the Alzheimer's Disease Education and Referral Center offers information on diagnosis, treatment, patient care, caregiver needs, long-term care, education, and research related to Alzheimer's disease.

## Association for Frontotemporal Dementias (AFTD)

1616 Walnut Street, Suite 1100
Philadelphia, PA 19103
(267) 514-7221
www.FTD-Picks.org
info@FTD-Picks.org

The Association for Frontotemporal Dementias is a nation-wide organization whose mission is to promote and support research into finding the cause and cure for frontotemporal dementias (FTD); to provide information, education, and support to people diagnosed with FTD and their families and caregivers; and to educate physicians and other health professionals about FTD.

## Batten Disease Support and Research Association

166 Humphries Drive
Reynoldsburg, OH 43068
(800) 448-4570
www.bdsra.org
nurse@bdsra.org

The Batten Disease Support and Research Association exists as an international support and research organization for families of children with Batten disease.

## Family Caregiver Alliance

180 Montgomery Street, Suite 1100
San Francisco, CA 94104
(415) 434-3388
www.caregiver.org
info@caregiver.org

The mission of the Family Caregiver Alliance is to improve the quality of life for caregivers through education, services, research, and support.

# Lewy Body Dementia Association

PO Box 451429
Atlanta, GA 31145
(800) 539-9767
www.lewybodydementia.org
lbda@lbda.org

The Lewy Body Dementia Association is dedicated to raising awareness of the Lewy body dementias; supporting patients, their families and caregivers; and promoting scientific advances.

# For Further Reading

## Books

Linda Jacobs Altman, *Alzheimer's Disease*. San Diego, CA: Lucent Books, 2001. A thorough treatment of Alzheimer's disease, its diagnosis, treatment, and management.

Frank Broyles, *Coach Broyles' Playbook for Alzheimer's Caregivers*. Alzheimer's Association, 2006. A cleverly designed, spiral-bound book that looks like a coach's playbook, written for caregivers by Frank Broyles, the athletic director for the University of Arkansas.

Margaret O. Hyde and John F. Setaro, *When the Brain Dies First*. New York: Franklin Watts, 2000. An easy-to-read description of brain injury and illness, including several types of dementia.

Connie McIntyre, *Flowers for Grandpa Dan: A Gentle Story to Help Children Understand Alzheimer's Disease*. St. Louis, MO: Thumbprint Press, 2005. The account of a child coping with the loss of his beloved grandfather to Alzheimer's disease. Good for younger readers.

Margeret Shawver, *What's Wrong with Grandma? A Family's Experience with Alzheimer's*. Amherst, NY: Prometheus, 1996. The story of a family's struggle with Alzheimer's disease, told from the point of view of a young girl. Good for young readers.

Edward Willett, *Alzheimer's Disease*. Berkeley Heights, NJ: Enslow, 2002. A comprehensive look at Alzheimer's disease.

## Web Sites

About.com (www.about.com). A multifaceted, searchable Web site for finding out about a multitude of health topics.

eMedicineHealth.com (www.emedicinehealth.com). Searchable site for learning about many health topics.

**Medline Plus** (www.medlineplus.gov). Health information on many topics from the National Library of Medicine.

**National Institute of Mental Health, National Institutes of Health** (www.nimh.nih.gov). Searchable Web site for learning about all types of mental illnesses.

**UCSF Memory and Aging Center** (www.memory.ucsf.edu). This site provides educational information about many kinds of dementia and other age-related disorders.

# Index

# Picture Credits

# About the Author

Lizabeth Hardman received her bachelor of science in nursing from the University of Florida in 1978 and her bachelor of secondary education from Southwest Missouri State University in 1991. She currently works full time as a surgical nurse, specializing in general and vascular surgery.

Hardman has published both fiction and nonfiction for adults and children. She especially enjoys writing about history, biography, and medical topics. She lives in Springfield, Missouri, with her two daughters, Rebecca and Wendy; two dogs; two cats; five birds; and one (very nice) python. When she is not working or writing, she enjoys reading, hiking, and St. Louis Cardinals baseball. *Dementia* is her fourth book for Lucent Books.